U.S.-MEXICO TRANSBOUNDARY HYDROCARBONS AGREEMENT

CONSIDERATIONS AND IMPLEMENTATION PROPOSALS

LATIN AMERICAN POLITICAL, ECONOMIC, AND SECURITY ISSUE

Additional books in this series can be found on Nova's website
under the Series tab.

Additional E-books in this series can be found on Nova's website
under the E-book tab.

LATIN AMERICAN POLITICAL, ECONOMIC, AND SECURITY ISSUES

U.S.-MEXICO TRANSBOUNDARY HYDROCARBONS AGREEMENT

CONSIDERATIONS AND IMPLEMENTATION PROPOSALS

HUGH BRUNER
EDITOR

New York

For permission to use material from this book please contact us:
Telephone 631-231-7269; Fax 631-231-8175
Web Site: http://www.novapublishers.com

NOTICE TO THE READER

The Publisher has taken reasonable care in the preparation of this book, but makes no expressed or implied warranty of any kind and assumes no responsibility for any errors or omissions. No liability is assumed for incidental or consequential damages in connection with or arising out of information contained in this book. The Publisher shall not be liable for any special, consequential, or exemplary damages resulting, in whole or in part, from the readers' use of, or reliance upon, this material. Any parts of this book based on government reports are so indicated and copyright is claimed for those parts to the extent applicable to compilations of such works.

Independent verification should be sought for any data, advice or recommendations contained in this book. In addition, no responsibility is assumed by the publisher for any injury and/or damage to persons or property arising from any methods, products, instructions, ideas or otherwise contained in this publication.

This publication is designed to provide accurate and authoritative information with regard to the subject matter covered herein. It is sold with the clear understanding that the Publisher is not engaged in rendering legal or any other professional services. If legal or any other expert assistance is required, the services of a competent person should be sought. FROM A DECLARATION OF PARTICIPANTS JOINTLY ADOPTED BY A COMMITTEE OF THE AMERICAN BAR ASSOCIATION AND A COMMITTEE OF PUBLISHERS.

Additional color graphics may be available in the e-book version of this book.

LIBRARY OF CONGRESS CATALOGING-IN-PUBLICATION DATA

ISBN: 978-1-63117-307-3

Published by Nova Science Publishers, Inc. † New York

CONTENTS

PREFACE

This book discusses the legislation proposal of implementing the U.S.-Mexico Transboundary Hydrocarbons Agreement. Another topic discussed in the book is the oil in Mexico in regards to the Transboundary Agreement. Mexican hydrocarbon resources belong to the Mexican people. Popular enthusiasm and national pride is attached to those resources, and many Mexicans directly depend on the existing oil industry for their livelihood and business interests. Crossing into the territory of energy sector reform requires political courage on behalf of Mexican politicians. The United States government emphatically recognizes the privileged position of oil in Mexico's politics.

Chapter 1 – The offshore areas of the Gulf of Mexico provide a setting for domestic and international energy production, U.S. military training and border operations, trade and commerce, fishing, tourist attractions, and recreation. These governmental, commercial, and cultural activities depend on healthy and productive marine and coastal areas for a range of economic and social benefits. Consequences of hurricanes and oil spills demonstrate that offshore areas in the Gulf of Mexico are governed by a number of interrelated legal regimes, including treaties and international, federal, and state laws.

A key congressional interest has been the federal role in managing energy resources in deepwater areas of the Gulf of Mexico, particularly in waters beyond the U.S. exclusive economic zone (EEZ), more than 200 miles from shore. In 2012, the United States and Mexico signed an agreement known as the U.S.-Mexico Transboundary Hydrocarbons Agreement (the Agreement). This Agreement could mark the start of an energy partnership in an area of international waters that the U.S. Department of the Interior's (DOI's) Bureau of Ocean Energy Management (BOEM) estimates to contain as much as 172 million barrels of oil and 304 billion cubic feet of natural gas. The main purposes of the partnership would be to lift a moratorium and to jointly develop reservoirs of oil and natural gas, referred to as "transboundary resources," that exist in areas straddling the marine border of both countries. The Agreement stems from a series of bilateral treaties originating in the 1970s. Like other diplomatic measures, for the Agreement to take effect, it must be placed before each country's national lawmakers for review. To date, Mexico has completed review and accepted the Agreement. The Agreement awaits the passage of implementing legislation in the U.S. Congress.

Chapter 2 – Relations Committee, requested senior professional staff members to review opportunities for enhanced U.S.-Mexico engagement on oil and gas issues including the U.S.-Mexico Transboundary Agreement, which requires Congressional action to take effect.

As part of that review, members of Senator Lugar's staff traveled to Mexico City in October 2012 to meet with then President-elect Enrique Peña Nieto's transition team and leaders from the Mexican Congress, PEMEX, the Mexican energy regulator Comisión Nacional de Hidrocarburos, U.S. industry, academic specialists, and U.S. officials at Embassy Mexico City.[1] This report contains their public findings and recommendations.

Congressional attention to the Mexican energy situation is critical for understanding bilateral issues between our countries and for consideration of U.S. energy security.

The United States has a profound interest in economic prosperity and political stability in Mexico, and energy is foundational to both interests. Oil is vital for the Mexican federal budget, underwriting both social programs and law and order, and the oil industry is an important aspect of broader economic activity. Stability and growth, or lack thereof, in Mexico's oil and gas sector can directly impact issues of bilateral concern.

Chapter 3 – This is the Statement of Ambassador Carlos Pascual, Special Envoy and Coordinator for International Energy Affairs, U.S. Department of State.

Chapter 4 – This is the Statement of Steven Groves, Bernard and Barbara Lomas Senior Research Fellow, The Heritage Foundation.

Chapter 5 – This is the Testimony of Athan Manuel, Director, Lands Protection Program, Sierra Club.

In: U.S.-Mexico Transboundary Hydrocarbons ...   ISBN: 978-1-63117-307-3
Editor: Hugh Bruner   © 2014 Nova Science Publishers, Inc.

Chapter 1

LEGISLATION PROPOSED TO IMPLEMENT THE U.S.-MEXICO TRANSBOUNDARY HYDROCARBONS AGREEMENT[*]

Curry L. Hagerty and James C. Uzel

SUMMARY

The offshore areas of the Gulf of Mexico provide a setting for domestic and international energy production, U.S. military training and border operations, trade and commerce, fishing, tourist attractions, and recreation. These governmental, commercial, and cultural activities depend on healthy and productive marine and coastal areas for a range of economic and social benefits. Consequences of hurricanes and oil spills demonstrate that offshore areas in the Gulf of Mexico are governed by a number of interrelated legal regimes, including treaties and international, federal, and state laws.

A key congressional interest has been the federal role in managing energy resources in deepwater areas of the Gulf of Mexico, particularly in waters beyond the U.S. exclusive economic zone (EEZ), more than 200 miles from shore. In 2012, the United States and Mexico signed an agreement known as the U.S.-Mexico Transboundary Hydrocarbons Agreement (the Agreement). This Agreement could mark the start of an energy partnership in an area of

---

[*] This is an edited, reformatted and augmented version of a Congressional Research Service Publication, CRS Report for Congress R43204, dated November 6, 2013.

international waters that the U.S. Department of the Interior's (DOI's) Bureau of Ocean Energy Management (BOEM) estimates to contain as much as 172 million barrels of oil and 304 billion cubic feet of natural gas. The main purposes of the partnership would be to lift a moratorium and to jointly develop reservoirs of oil and natural gas, referred to as "transboundary resources," that exist in areas straddling the marine border of both countries. The Agreement stems from a series of bilateral treaties originating in the 1970s. Like other diplomatic measures, for the Agreement to take effect, it must be placed before each country's national lawmakers for review. To date, Mexico has completed review and accepted the Agreement. The Agreement awaits the passage of implementing legislation in the U.S. Congress.

In the United States, implementing legislation involves the two main commitments of the Agreement. First, under the Agreement, the two countries establish a framework for jointly developing 1.5 million acres along a 550-mile border. Diplomats on both sides of the border claim that this framework achieves a mutual goal of greater options for energy production to help gain greater energy independence for both countries. A concurrent commitment is to dismantle a treaty-based moratorium on oil and gas development agreed to in 2000, encompassing 158,584 acres along a 135-mile portion of the border. Current treaty provisions establish that the ban will expire in 2014.

Implementing the Agreement faces hurdles in both countries. In the United States, among other hurdles, is the transitional status of U.S. safety reforms announced after the 2010 Deepwater Horizon spill. These reforms are being phased in and full implementation is not anticipated until later in 2013 and 2014. These regulations are considered by industry and U.S. regulators to be a more robust set of deepwater drilling standards than were in place prior to the Deepwater Horizon spill. Until they take full effect, the treaty-based moratorium is perceived by many as a necessary mechanism to protect against the risk of oil spills. In Mexico, although the Agreement has been accepted, implementation poses various constitutional and regulatory challenges.

U.S. legislation to approve and implement the Agreement includes H.R. 1613 and S. 812. On June 27, 2013, the House passed H.R. 1613 (H.Rept. 113-101). On October 14, 2013, the Senate passed S. 812. Absent a deadline for U.S. approval of the Agreement and consideration of implementing legislation, if any, it is difficult to predict the timing of further legislative action. Many in Congress have expressed the view that the expiration of the moratorium in 2014 will prove a catalyst for legislative attention during the remainder of the 113th Congress.

INTRODUCTION

Since the 1970s, prompted by high fuel prices and a mutual interest in greater energy security, the United States and Mexico have agreed to a series of bilateral treaties defining territorial claims and laying the groundwork for future oil and gas development partnerships. These treaties and other diplomatic activities are helping to define each nation's stake in oil and gas resources in ocean areas in the western Gulf of Mexico beyond each country's 200-mile exclusive economic zone (EEZ).[1]

A prominent component of these treaties has been an offshore moratorium on oil and gas development covering a 158,584-acre area within a larger transboundary area encompassing 1.5 million acres.[2] The stated purpose of this moratorium is to allow time for both countries to form a partnership for jointly developing transboundary oil and gas resources beyond each country's EEZ.

The United States and Mexico are moving to form a partnership to jointly manage areas for offshore drilling operations. This entails lifting the temporary moratorium and replacing it with a framework for a joint development scenario.[3] The United States and Mexico are not alone in seeking this type of energy partnership. Around the world, nations claiming ocean areas beyond established national borders are forming similar partnerships to cope with challenges associated with managing offshore areas for developing oil and gas resources.[4] The global race for ocean energy resources is among other contributors to the intensification of diplomatic talks between the United States and Mexico that started in 2010. These talks were concluded in 2012 by both countries signing the U.S.-Mexico Transboundary Hydrocarbons Agreement (the Agreement).[5]

Several hurdles stand in the way of this energy partnership — each stemming from different policy dilemmas on each side of the border.[6] While the Mexican Senate moved swiftly to approve the Agreement on April 12, 2012, and the Mexican Presidency completed other domestic requirements on May 22, 2012, uncertainties surround Mexico's implementation of the Agreement. At issue is the role of Mexico's state oil company, PEMEX, specifically whether PEMEX is able to pursue deepwater operations without significant regulatory challenges.[7]

In contrast to the examination of issues underway in Mexico, the hurdle in the United States involves lack of consensus about lifting the moratorium. To date, the Bureau of Safety and Environmental Enforcement (BSEE) has not completed phasing in safety reforms promulgated by the agency in 2010 and 2011 in the wake of the Deepwater Horizon oil spill.[8] Without these new safety requirements (anticipated in later 2013 and 2014), there is little to counter concerns expressed by some U.S. interests dependent on water-related activities in the Gulf of Mexico (fishing, recreation, and tourism) that the moratorium is needed to prevent possible oil spill risks that can accompany deepwater drilling operations in the Gulf of Mexico.[9]

On February 20, 2012, at the signing ceremony for the Agreement, U.S. officials acknowledged that for the Agreement to take effect, both countries must review and accept it. Referring to the challenges facing the Agreement on both sides of the border, these officials praised the Agreement as a way to help both countries reach a mutual goal— improved North American energy security. Specifically, then-Secretary of State Hillary Rodham Clinton referred to "shared challenges" when announcing the Agreement: "Our actions today are further proof of how Mexico and the United States come together to solve shared challenges. From our earliest days, the Gulf of Mexico has been a source of unity for our peoples and our countries. And the steps we are taking today will help make sure it remains that way for decades to come."[10]

To date, U.S. review of the Agreement includes House and Senate passage of legislation to approve and implement the Agreement. On June 27, 2013, the House passed H.R. 1613 (H.Rept. 113-101); and on October 14, 2013, the Senate passed S. 812. Controversy surrounding House action highlighted a persistent tension between proponents of ocean oil and gas drilling seeking to accelerate production of domestic energy supplies and those who favor maintaining the moratorium in order to provide time for safety and environmental issues to be addressed.[11] The Senate passed S. 812 by unanimous consent. The legislation is discussed in greater detail below, in the section on "Pending Legislation and Related Legislative Interests."

Congress can act on the Agreement throughout the remainder of the 113th Congress, or can defer action indefinitely. While the Agreement awaits U.S. attention, the moratorium that was established in a previous treaty remains in effect until 2014, or until another acceptable alternative (diplomatic or legislative) supersedes it.

Recent Developments

Proposed legislation providing the Secretary of the Interior the authority to implement the Transboundary Agreement has passed in both chambers: (S. 812 passed in the Senate; H.R. 1613 passed in the House). Lawmakers favoring these bills express support for a goal found in both bills—providing congressional approval of the Agreement. Objections to the legislation were expressed by those in Congress opposed to provisions found only in H.R. 1613, as reported by the House Committee on Natural Resources. These provisions would exempt actions taken by public companies from requirements under a section of the Securities and Exchange Commission's Natural Resource Extraction Disclosure Rule. It is widely recognized that, among other provisions found in H.R. 1613, those clarifying this disclosure requirement involve issues beyond implementing the Agreement.

In both chambers, supporters and opponents have expressed an increased interest in legislation to achieve goals limited to approving and implementing the Agreement to establish a framework for the cooperative exploration and development of oil and gas reservoirs that cross the international maritime boundary in the Gulf of Mexico. While opponents express specific objections to certain provisions aimed at other objectives (found in H.R. 1613,[12] but not in S. 812), committee chairs and ranking members in both chambers have pledged expeditious approval of proposed implementing legislation. Legislative action is discussed in greater detail below.

Policy Review: U.S. Offshore Oil and Gas Leasing System

In its current form, the federally regulated offshore oil and gas leasing system comprises roughly 1.7 billion acres beyond state waters, including the U.S. exclusive economic zone (EEZ) and areas beyond the U.S. EEZ.[13] Responsibility for managing ocean energy resources falls within the U.S. Department of State and the U.S. Department of the Interior's (DOI's) Bureau of Ocean Energy Management (BOEM).[14] Conveying U.S. leases through lease sales and managing the leasing system (from early planning to decommissioning) is achieved mainly through the Five- Year Outer Continental Shelf Oil and Gas Leasing Program[15] and the Offshore Renewable Energy Program.[16] Consistent with the objectives of each program, BOEM manages more than 8,000 active leases organized in a grid system that was established at the start of the program in 1953.[17]

U.S. ocean energy production currently accounts for 26% of domestic oil production and about 16% of domestic natural gas production. While most offshore acreage is found in the Alaska region (approximately 1.03 billion acres of a total of 1.7 billion acres), oil and gas leases are located mainly in the Gulf of Mexico (89% of the federally regulated offshore energy activity is concentrated in an area accounting for about 2% of U.S. waters). **Figure 1** illustrates generally where U.S. oil and gas lease sales take place in the Gulf of Mexico.

Specifically, **Figure 1** depicts ocean areas in the Gulf of Mexico in relation to coastal states and cities, highlighting areas eligible for lease sales (shaded areas) and areas ineligible for lease sales (unshaded areas).[18] In addition to generating domestic energy supplies in these areas, federally regulated offshore energy projects are recognized as generating significant public receipts, including approximately $6.9 billion in 2012.[19] U.S. lease sales in the Gulf of Mexico resulted in reported revenues totaling over $13 billion in the last two years.[20] DOI estimates future revenues of $50 million in 2014 from energy activities projected to take place in the transboundary area if the Agreement is accepted and implemented.[21]

National ownership and use of ocean resources are issues attracting increased attention in Congress, particularly when they involve transboundary areas of international waters.[22] Competing national interests in offshore drilling stir questions: How does Congress balance the nation's interests in resource use and protection in international ocean areas? What are effective ways to monitor safety at international marine borders, particularly when the marine areas fall under the jurisdiction of multiple federal agencies?[23] Some in Congress have expressed an interest in these questions through legislative proposals, program oversight, and annual appropriations for the relevant federal agencies.

U.S.-Mexico Transboundary Hydrocarbons Agreement

The Agreement is widely recognized as an initial step toward a joint development scenario involving three U.S.-Mexico commitments: (1) eliminating the moratorium in waters beyond their respective exclusive economic zones (EEZs); (2) studying the transboundary areas (exchanging geological information); and (3) potentially deploying joint oil and gas operations associated with developing transboundary reservoirs.[24]

Under the current statutory framework, U.S. commitments fall into three basic categories: commitments relative to federal-state coordination[25] (mainly to recognize state policies in state waters); commitments that are federal in nature[26] (mainly balancing competing energy and environmental interests at the national level); and commitments relative to the international context[27] (a fluid mix of military, trade, and diplomatic missions derived unilaterally or through nation-to-nation mechanisms). Given the fragmented and overlapping nature of these three categories, several questions have arisen related to how U.S. commitments under the Agreement might affect U.S. interests. Would the Agreement lead to any new legal or regulatory obligations for U.S. interests? Would existing environmental laws or existing lease terms and conditions in effect in the Gulf of Mexico be affected by the Agreement? What, if any, fiscal implications might result from carrying out collaborative projects in the boundary area?

PENDING LEGISLATION AND RELATED LEGISLATIVE INTERESTS

The Administration and some in and outside of Congress have advocated for swift U.S. review and acceptance of the Agreement. Others have expressed skepticism that the Agreement is an optimal approach to expand the ocean energy portfolio in the Gulf of Mexico. Two legislative initiatives (H.R. 1613 and S. 812) were introduced as part of the U.S. review of the Agreement. Each bill would accept the Agreement, taking a slightly different approach to implementation.

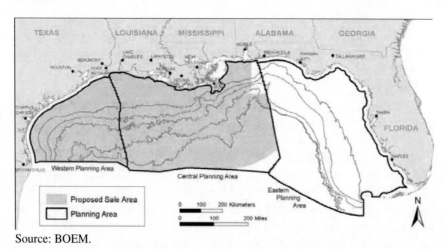

Source: BOEM.

Figure 1. U.S. Gulf of Mexico in Relation to Selected Coastal States and Cities.

H.R. 1613

H.R. 1613, "Outer Continental Shelf Transboundary Hydrocarbon Agreements Authorization Act," was considered and passed by the House on June 27, 2013.[28] This legislation would establish guidelines and procedures for implementing the Agreement; and among other measures, would provide for legislative review of any future agreements governing that area. The bill would amend the Outer Continental Shelf Lands Act (OCSLA, 43 U.S.C. 1331 et seq.) to implement the Agreement by providing new powers to the Secretary of the Interior for approving unitization agreements.[29]

By adding a new section to the end of the OCSLA ("Section 32"), the bill authorizes the Secretary to implement the Agreement with Mexico by completing the following steps:

- submitting the Agreement to the Speaker of the House; the Majority Leader of the Senate; the Chairs of the House Committee on Natural Resources and the Senate Committee on Energy and Natural Resources;
- including in the submission (1) legislation relevant to implementation; (2) economic analysis of impacts of the Agreement on domestic production of offshore oil and gas resources; (3) a description of regulations expected to be issued to implement the Agreement; and (4) provisions adopting unitization as the approach to developing the area.[30]

Furthermore, H.R. 1613 would exempt U.S. firms from certain reporting requirements of the Securities Exchange Act of 1934.[31] Currently, publicly traded companies are required to disclose certain information regarding business dealings related to extractive operations to investors through filings with the Securities and Exchange Commission (SEC). Section 1504 of the Dodd- Frank Wall Street Reform and Consumer Protection Act of 2010 (P.L. 111-203) amended the Securities Exchange Act of 1934 by expanding certain required public company disclosures.[32] When applied to the commercial development of oil, natural gas, or minerals, the act requires the disclosure of certain payments made to the federal government or foreign governments by public companies required to file annual reports with the SEC. The provision in H.R. 1613 entitled "Exemption from Resources Extraction" provides that actions taken by such a public company pertaining to any transboundary hydrocarbon agreement shall be exempt from such disclosure requirements.[33]

S. 812[34]

This bill would authorize the Secretary of the Interior to implement the Agreement in a manner consistent with legislative provisions proposed by the Administration and referred to in the Administration's 2014 budget request.[35] Specifically, under the legislative proposal referred to in the budget request and under S. 812, the Secretary of the Interior is provided with new authorities to approve unitization agreements and related arrangements within certain guidelines. This approach contrasts with H.R. 1613 in several respects.

A key distinction between the Senate and House bills is the additional provisions in the House bill, particularly regarding disclosure requirements for investment information pursuant to U.S. Securities and Exchange Commission (SEC) rules. Specifically, the House bill clarifies the application of Section 13(q) of the Securities Exchange Act of 1934[36] in matters related to joint development projects in the transboundary area. In contrast, S. 812 is silent on this point, not addressing the treatment of U.S. firms and SEC obligations.

Related Legislative Interests

Congressional interests relevant to U.S. legislative implementation of this Agreement include the following:

- **Hearings Addressing a Range of Public Lands Issues**. Multiple oversight hearings in the House and Senate during the 113th Congress have involved lawmakers examining how current federal resource management laws govern energy production. These hearings reflect two visions: seeing the need to grant access to some areas to enhance energy production and —as a counterbalance— seeing the need to defer access to some areas to protect people and the environment from risk. As part of hearings about offshore energy development, some Members are proposing statutory changes related to the following: (1) alternatives to current programs for allocating federal receipts generated from drilling operations and offshore wind farms; (2) deployment of more diverse ocean energy technologies in a wider range of locations; and (3) changes in the pace of inspections and permitting. To date, legislative attention to these various themes demonstrates that lawmakers are considering statutory changes by addressing the U.S. offshore energy program as a whole. In contrast to piecemeal approaches of the past, there seems to be an interest in examining a broad agenda of interlocking issues to achieve a more diverse U.S. portfolio in the Gulf of Mexico and beyond.

- **Regulatory Actions to Solicit Bids for Ocean Tracts in the Transboundary Area**. As part of periodically conducting U.S. lease sales to convey development rights in ocean tracts in the Gulf of Mexico, BOEM has offered leases for oil and gas development rights pursuant to treaty terms established in 2000. As in the past, BOEM has announced that any bids on the transboundary area would not be opened until after both parties have accepted the Agreement. Specifically, as part of offering offshore oil and gas development rights beyond the U.S. EEZ and near the marine boundary area with Mexico, in 2012 BOEM conducted Sale 229,[40] and in 2013, Sale 233.[41] Agency preparation for these lease sales has included offering maps of offshore areas depicting where the U.S. grid is located with respect to leased and unleased tracts and stipulating certain lease terms and conditions related to tracts in the transboundary area.

WHAT, IF ANYTHING, HAS CHANGED SINCE THE GULF OIL SPILL OF 2010?

In the aftermath of the April 20, 2010, explosion and fire on the *Deepwater Horizon*[37] in the Gulf of Mexico, federal regulators reexamined some of the risks and benefits accompanying deepwater drilling, bolstered enforcement measures related to operational safety, and revised standards for certain deepwater drilling operations.

Perceptions about the adequacy of these federal reforms vary. As implementation of these reforms continues to unfold, some in Congress have expressed an interest in how the reforms might be affecting energy production, worker safety, and environmental protection in U.S. waters.[38]

More than one Government Accountability Office (GAO) study is underway to offer insights on DOI agency performance as part of a broader look at how federal offshore areas are managed.[39]

- **Diplomatic Cooperation on Oil Spill Risks**. For decades, U.S.-Mexico cooperation on oil spill risks has included planning strategies to cope with pollution caused by oil spills. Both countries participate regularly in a joint contingency planning in order to ensure adequate response to spills.[42] The current joint plan—known as Mexus Plan—sets standard operating procedures in case of incidents that threaten the coastal waters or marine environment of the border zone of both countries. The U.S. response team is coordinated by the Coast Guard's Assistant Commandant for Marine Safety and Environmental Protection.[43]

RELEVANT GEOGRAPHIC AREAS

The Agreement reflects a continued commitment by the United States and Mexico to identify and define certain geographic areas located beyond each country's EEZ. These areas were first recognized by both countries through diplomatic channels in 1978. **Figure 2** illustrates these areas in relation to U.S.-Mexico treaty lines.[44]

The recognition by the United States and Mexico of certain geographic areas located beyond each country's EEZ is consistent with customary international law relevant to countries planning to regulate drilling operations beyond their EEZs. Areas beyond the U.S.-Mexico EEZs are largely unexamined for oil and gas development. As a result, there is not a robust collection of data about impacts of energy development on particular populations and ecosystems. Both countries' diplomats have stated plans to monitor activities taking place in transboundary areas as a component of a joint development scenario.

The line-striped areas depicted in **Figure 2** illustrate areas defined by treaty. These areas are sometimes referred to as "gaps" (specifically the "Western Gap" and the "Eastern Gap"). This signifies not only a gap that exists in how nations define the legal status of that area, but also a gap in available scientific information about the area.

Western Gap

The Western Gap is the polygon located in **Figure 2** in the western portion of the Gulf of Mexico and in **Figure 3** as the main image. The Western Gap encompasses about 4.2 million acres. Although the Western Gap falls outside both the U.S. and Mexico EEZs, most of the acreage is recognized as belonging to either the United States or Mexico, while a certain portion falls along the transboundary line between U.S. and Mexican waters. The U.S.

acreage in the Western Gap includes about 1.5 million acres to the north of the transboundary area.[45] Of the U.S. acreage within the Western Gap, the portion falling in the transboundary area and covered by the moratorium measures 158,584 acres. Some ocean acreage in the U.S. portion of the Western Gap (other than the transboundary area covered by moratorium) has been offered at U.S. lease sales since 2001.[46]

Transboundary Area

The transboundary area defined in the Agreement is illustrated in **Figure 4** as a solid yellow line running east beyond Texas state waters, through the Western Gap, to the western edge of the Eastern Gap. As discussed above, the U.S. portion of this area encompasses 1.5 million acres, located in a corridor also referred to as the Delimitation Line.

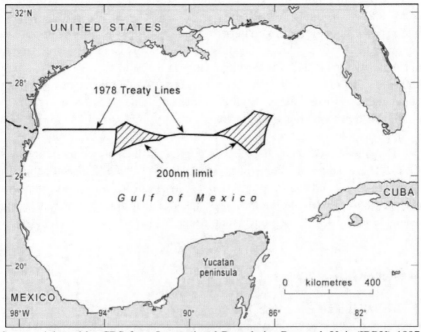

Source: Adapted by CRS from International Boundaries Research Unit (IBRU) 1997. Line-striped areas are the western and eastern polygons representing "gaps" where national marine boundaries have not been fully defined.

Figure 2. Basic Features of the Western and Eastern Gaps in the Gulf of Mexico.

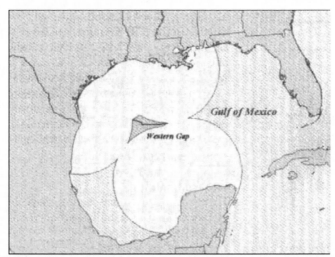

Source: CRS modifications to image available from National Geodetic Survey (NGS)
    National Ocean Service (NOS) National Oceanic and Atmospheric Administration
    (NOAA) at http://www.ngs.noaa.gov/CORS/Articles/ solgps.pdf.

Figure 3. Detail of Western Gap in the Gulf of Mexico Showing U.S. and Mexico
EEZ.

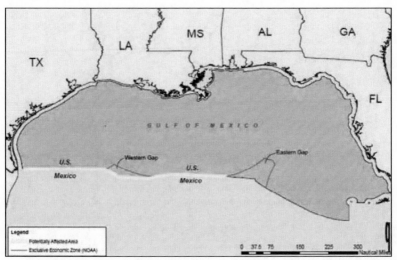

Source: BOEM. U.S. side of the Western Gap (1.5 million U.S. acres) and the Eastern
    Gap (undetermined U.S. acreage) is shown. Mexican coastal areas are not shown.

Figure 4. Delimitation Line Defined by the Agreement.

Moratorium Area

The moratorium area is located entirely inside the Western Gap, along the transboundary line. It comprises a narrow (2.8 nautical miles) corridor cutting across a 135-mile distance (158,584 acres).[47] The moratorium area attracts attention, partly because, as **Figure 5** illustrates, it is located in a mid-section of the 550-mile transboundary area.

Consistent with U.S.-Mexico treaty provisions, this moratorium expires in 2014. In the absence of applicable measures to the contrary, and absent clearance to lift the ban pursuant to the Agreement, the following actions are possible: allowing the moratorium to expire without further indication of international relations relative to managing the area; extending the moratorium for an agreeable time frame; or replacing the moratorium with some other alternative to which the United States and Mexico may need to agree.

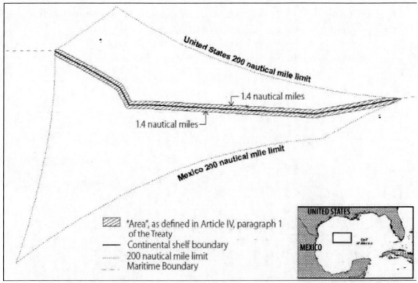

Source: CRS, adapted from the treaty documents submitted by U.S. negotiators in support of *Treaty between the Government of the United Mexican States and the Government of the United States of America on the Continental Shelf* signed on June 9, 2000.

Figure 5. Illustration of the Moratorium Area Located in the Western Gap.

Upon signing the Agreement, U.S. negotiators elaborated on various diplomatic activities, including plans to eliminate the moratorium after review and acceptance of the Agreement by both countries.[48] Further commitments included providing U.S. leaseholders with a framework for exploiting transboundary reservoirs through "unitization";[49] encouraging options for investment; offering predictable resolution of disputes; and ensuring a joint safety regime.[50] These commitments spark a tension between the perceived need to commence oil and gas operations and the notion that deferring such operations through the moratorium would provide more time to resolve domestic regulatory policy dilemmas. This tension is discussed in the section "Issues for Congress."

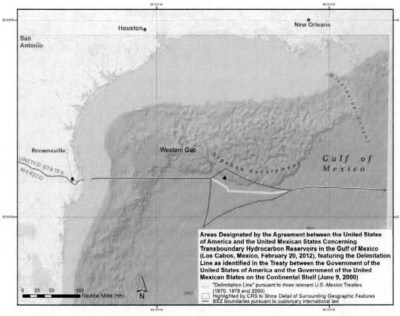

Source: CRS.

Notes: CRS designed this image to feature lines detailed in the Agreement. Specifically, CRS used point data from the Treaty between the Government of the United States of America and the Government of the United Mexican States on the Delimitation of the Continental Shelf in the Western Gulf of Mexico beyond 200 Nautical Miles, June 9, 2000. This image also features locations of the Sigsbee Escarpment and the Mississippi Canyon, not detailed in the Treaty or depicted in other images in this report.

Figure 6. Selected Features of the Transboundary Area.

CONCISE SUMMARY OF THE AGREEMENT[51]

This section introduces readers to the contents of the Agreement by summarizing some major concepts found in all seven chapters and 27 articles. Provisions attracting particular attention include Chapter 3 (Articles 10-13: establishing a joint development scenario) and Chapter 7 (Article 24: terminating the current moratorium).

Chapter 1 (Articles 1-5) describes the "General Principles" of the Agreement including the scope,[52] definitions,[53] jurisdiction[54] and activities near the Delimitation Line.[55] Furthermore, this chapter establishes a process for jointly determining the existence of transboundary reservoirs.[56]

Chapter 2 (Articles 6-9) outlines joint guidelines for companies from both countries to jointly explore and develop transboundary resources cited in the Agreement. These guidelines entail a "Unitization Agreement;"[57] joint management principles;[58] and production allocations.[59]

Chapter 3 (Articles 10-13) establishes requirements related to agreements involving unit operators.[60] It states broad guidelines addressing commercial aspects of the following: operations subject to a unit operation agreement[61] and fiscal terms related to exploiting oil and natural gas reservoirs in specific areas.[62]

Chapter 4 (Article 14) creates an institutional body for resolving disputes. This body is referred to as a Joint Commission.[63]

Chapter 5 (Articles 15-17) details the process for dispute settlement by providing options for parties to resolve disagreements arising from implementation of the Agreement.[64]

Chapter 6 (Articles 18-19) outlines principles for joint inspections relating to safety and environmental protection.[65]

Chapter 7 (Articles 20-27) concludes the Agreement with a variety of provisions to guide the process for amending, terminating and bringing the Agreement into force,[66] terminating the moratorium[67] and determining how the Agreement might relate to other agreements.[68]

Consistent with both countries' stated intentions in 2010,[69] officials on both sides of the border have asserted that the Agreement achieves stated goals for "jointly managing, administering and governing" the transboundary area in a "considered, sustainable and structured manner" in order to "optimize energy resource development and to protect the surrounding marine environment."[70]

POSSIBLE IMPLICATIONS OF IMPLEMENTING LEGISLATION[71]

Diplomats from the United States and Mexico have described possible implications of the Agreement entering into force as follows:

- The current moratorium on oil exploration and production would end.
- A cooperative process for managing the maritime boundary region would begin.
- It would be possible for commercial activities to unfold involving options for companies to voluntarily enter into unitization arrangements. In the event such an arrangement is not achieved, the Agreement also establishes options by which companies might develop potential resources on each side of the border.
- Joint inspection teams addressing compliance with applicable laws and regulations would be activated by both governments to review operational plans relevant to transboundary reservoirs.[72]

Parties on both sides of the border have observed that the Agreement does not provide specific details about a possible development scenario. Instead it offers a framework for both countries to work further to commence joint operations.

Other possible impacts on activities in the Gulf of Mexico or, from a broader perspective, on the national ocean energy portfolio remain a matter of conjecture.[73] For example, as part of estimating fiscal impacts, many in Congress turn to the Congressional Budget Office (CBO) score for H.R. 1613.[74]

On May 17, 2013, CBO estimated that "enacting H.R. 1613 would increase offsetting receipts from offshore lease sales by $25 million from 2014 through 2023." As part of this analysis, CBO assumes, first, that approving the Agreement would allow DOI to offer leases for acreage which is currently under moratorium and, second, that approving the Agreement would increase values of other leased tracts in the nearby area.[75]

Other possible implications of the Agreement coming into force involve coping with challenges related to safety and monitoring marine borders; issues surrounding disbursement of potential revenue anticipated from U.S.-Mexico projects; and the concentration of undeveloped leases in the Gulf of Mexico. Each of these issues is discussed in the next section.

WHAT IS "UNITIZATION?"

Unitization is a method to jointly develop a field or reservoir that might encompass a large area and even straddle a state or national boundary.

This method for OCS development is common in U.S. waters. Described by some as the centerpiece of the Agreement, unitization facilitates companies licensed by the United States and by Mexico (through the state oil company Petróleos Mexicanos, PEMEX) to operate as one entity as part of joint operations involving distinct oil and gas reservoirs potentially discovered to extend across the maritime boundary.[76] Frameworks for unitization (including the framework adopted in the U.S.-Mexico Agreement) can be founded on a combination of the following:

- international law—formal agreements between countries (consistent with treaties, conventions and international customs);
- national laws of host governments, and contracts between host governments and licensees; and
- private contracts among licensees and interested third parties, such as operating agreements and production sales contracts.

An example of a project in U.S. waters made possible through unitization exists in the western Gulf of Mexico—the Perdido project. **Figure 7** illustrates this project by highlighting the three subsea units that tie back to a floating production facility referred to as a Regional Host. This facility is located in approximately 8,000 feet of water, approximately 250 miles south of Houston, TX, and less than 100 miles from the transboundary area cited in the Agreement. When first constructed, this project was the deepest "vertical access" facility in the world.[77]

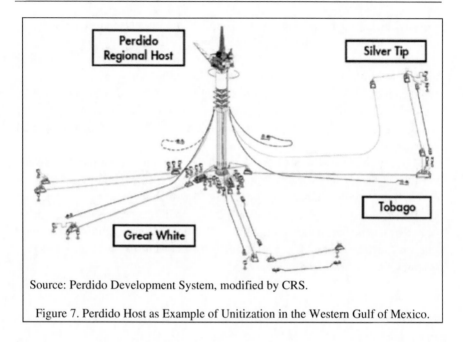

Source: Perdido Development System, modified by CRS.

Figure 7. Perdido Host as Example of Unitization in the Western Gulf of Mexico.

U.S. PERSPECTIVES AND ISSUES FOR CONGRESS

A number of developments have influenced review of the Agreement and subsequent legislative action by the 113th Congress. First, both governments have demonstrated an increased interest in developing ocean energy resources.[78] Second, the Mexican Senate moved swiftly to approve the Agreement on April 12, 2012, and the Mexican Presidency completed all other domestic requirements to implement the Agreement on May 22, 2012. Third, various U.S. stakeholders (some in the U.S. energy sector and some environmental organizations) have expressed interests related to the Agreement.[79] Further legislative action to implement the Agreement, if any, during the 113th Congress will likely also be influenced by the issues discussed below.

Jointly Developing Ocean Energy Resources

Many Members of Congress and the Obama Administration have supported efforts to enhance U.S.-Mexico energy cooperation for several reasons, including enhancing energy supplies and energy security. Executive branch officials assert that U.S. interests benefit from jointly developing the transboundary area, particularly in light of Mexico's role as a key U.S. partner in other policy spheres (trade, border issues, international drug interdiction and law enforcement). They also assert that U.S.-Mexico cooperation will help manage ocean energy resources on both sides of the marine border by enhancing energy production while monitoring safety and environmental protection.

U.S. diplomatic officials have asserted that various commitments between the United States and Mexico protect U.S. interests in expanding options for developing hydrocarbons and that this Agreement merely updates and strengthens existing treaties between the two countries. At issue for some in Congress is whether implementing this U.S.-Mexico Agreement is an essential step in forming U.S.-Mexico partnerships relevant to generating energy supplies along marine borders.

Disbursement of Revenue Anticipated from U.S.-Mexico Projects

U.S. officials usually seek to clarify the management of receipts and disbursements related to energy production as part of the earliest deliberations about options for developing ocean energy resources.[80]

Consistent with various revenue management mechanisms that have evolved over the years, an established percentage of federal revenues flows to federal and state projects in designated portions of the Gulf of Mexico.[81] In the past, determining an acceptable division of revenue from future offshore energy projects between coastal states and the federal government has proven to be a difficult problem. When leased tracts on federal territory are at issue, coastal states argue that they bear the brunt of remediating environmental impacts and infrastructure wear-and-tear accompanying offshore oil and gas activity. Some states also harbor concern about international development scenarios impacting shore-side communities and possibly increasing statewide costs related to water-dependent activities.

To date, OCS revenues have been a major source of funds for the Land and Water Conservation Fund (LWCF) and the National Historic Preservation Fund (NHPF).[82] State and federal entities use these funds to acquire park and recreational lands. Thus far, U.S. review of the Agreement has not examined values involved in an equitable distribution of public revenues, if any, related to offshore projects managed jointly by the United States and Mexico.

At issue for Congress is whether statutory mandates related to nation-to-nation or federal-state revenue-sharing programs might be considered as part of U.S. review of the Agreement.

Worker Safety, Public Health, and Environmental Protection

Worker safety, public health, and environmental protection stemming from activities at marine border areas present special challenges, in part because international marine borders tend to be geographically remote, resulting in limited options for equipment inspections, audits of worker training, and law enforcement coverage.[83] These concerns about activities in offshore areas are relevant to safety, health, and environmental protection issues onshore because of the nature of air- and waterborne pollutants and debris. At marine border areas, oil and gas facilities are subject to regulation by the Bureau of Safety and Environmental Enforcement (BSEE), the DOI agency responsible for federal inspections and reviewing oil spill response plans; and testing oil spill containment equipment.[84]

While marine border activities may be governed by different federal missions (military, diplomatic, trade) and involve various federal or international jurisdictions, agencies have been required to integrate planning and regulatory compliance requirements to ensure that federal decisions reflect values Americans place on worker safety and environmental protection.[85] Sometimes departments—including DOI, for example—have signed memoranda of understanding (MOUs) on border issues that govern information sharing related to safety, budgeting, and access to federal lands, among other topics.[86]

Of particular interest to some in Congress might be how legislative initiatives discussed above might ensure safety at the marine border by detailing strategies to address worker safety and environmental protection.

Concentration of Non-Producing Leases in the Gulf of Mexico

Continuous federal oil and gas leasing in the Gulf of Mexico from the 1950s to the present has contributed to a higher concentration of federal leases in the Gulf of Mexico region than in the other three regions (Atlantic, Pacific and Alaska) combined. DOI reports that most federally regulated leases in the Gulf of Mexico remain undeveloped (showing no physical signs of development). While the leases might generate rental receipts and values related to assignments and transfers, currently these leases generate neither energy supplies nor royalties.[87]

An issue attracting increased attention among some in Congress is how to cope with new leasing options when so many leased tracts already exist. Some concerned about the number of non- producing U.S. leases question the benefits of leasing more acreage without examining the significance, if any, of the backlog of undeveloped leased tracts. Others contend that with no statutory limit on the number of undeveloped leases a leaseholder may own, there should be no correlation between new leasing options and efforts to examine (or reduce) the number of non-producing leases.

Disagreements related to so-called "idle leases" can stem from differing perspectives on the values attached to the oil and gas leasing system in the U.S. Gulf of Mexico. Arguably, the value of each lease (producing and non-producing) is determined by the company owning the lease. In theory, all leases might play a role on an owner's balance sheet. Some leases might not be producing energy supplies or public revenue, but they provide operational and investment options for the leaseholder. These options that might include rights-of-way, access to credit through liens or mortgages, or other attributes derived from accounting rules or the tax code.[88]

Attention to this issue has a tendency to wax and wane, with lawmaker interest increasing in recent years.

CONCLUSION

Controversy surrounds most U.S. legislative initiatives to grant (or defer) offshore oil and gas drilling rights. A persistent question among lawmakers is how to cope with myriad issues and competing interests at stake when it comes to managing ocean resources.[89] Of the breadth of issues and interests that might be related to proposed legislation to implement the U.S.-Mexico Transboundary Hydrocarbons Agreement, this report focuses on resource management issues, only addressing the competing national interests that mainly involve balancing the demands of producing ocean energy supplies while protecting marine and coastal resources and resources found beyond the U.S. EEZ.

While the Obama Administration has stated that the Agreement is part of engaging Mexico in a host of related energy and environmental partnerships, asserting that the benefits of this Agreement outweigh potential risks, skeptics have voiced doubt that the Agreement ensures an emphasis on rigorous safety measures on both sides of the border.[90] Related issues include how to handle public receipts (royalties and other gains), if any, anticipated from jointly managed ocean energy projects and how to cope with oil spill risks and other risks associated with a joint development scenario.

Recent activities in the House and Senate highlight increased interest in implementing the Agreement. In the House, debate underscored a policy divide that accompanies legislative review of this Agreement.[91] Arguably, positions expressed about legislation to accept and implement the Agreement reflect two camps: one focusing on the benefits of maintaining the moratorium on ocean drilling and the other focusing on gains anticipated from options to generate new energy supplies and public revenues.

Some of these arguments highlight external factors associated with U.S.-Mexico relations.[92] However, most arguments are reminiscent of the historic choices faced by U.S. lawmakers in the past about whether and where to allow ocean drilling and how to monitor development scenarios where permissible.

As the expiration of the moratorium draws closer, pressure may increase for lawmakers and diplomatic officials on both sides of the border to find an acceptable policy alternative for achieving a safe, responsible, and sustainable future for U.S. and Mexican ocean energy portfolios in the Gulf of Mexico. With no schedule in place for further U.S. review of the Agreement, it is difficult to predict whether Congress might defer attention to the Agreement or undertake further U.S. review.

APPENDIX. SUMMARY OF CONGRESSIONAL HEARINGS

Both House hearings discussed below were conducted prior to lawmakers introducing the bills discussed elsewhere in this report. Absent the opportunity to parse introduced legislation, witnesses mainly offered general statements relevant to the Agreement. As a result these hearings were free of the more precise legislative analysis and stakeholder discussion that can come from review directly related to pending legislation.[93]

House Committee on Foreign Affairs

On March 14, 2013, the House Committee on Foreign Affairs, Subcommittee on the Western Hemisphere held a hearing entitled *U.S. Energy Security: Enhancing Partnerships with Mexico and Canada.*[94] At the hearing the four witnesses representing academia and private sector firms[95] claimed U.S. approval of the Agreement would impact U.S. and Mexican interests through one or more of the following considerations:

- "Approving the treaty will create new levels of legal certainty for U.S. and Mexican firms operating in the Gulf border regions, encouraging them to engage in the risk-taking required to produce oil from deep waters ... "[96]
- "Swift ratification of the Transboundary Hydrocarbon Agreement is important to our nation's energy security and long-term economic growth."[97]
- "The current focus on hydrocarbon reform in Mexico also means that extended U.S. inaction on the Transboundary Hydrocarbons Agreement will be noticed, with potentially negative consequences for the broader bilateral relationship."[98]

House Committee on Natural Resources

On April 25, 2013, the House Committee on Natural Resources, Subcommittee on Energy and Mineral Resources held a legislative and oversight hearing entitled *"U.S.-Mexico Transboundary Hydrocarbon Agreement and Steps Needed for Implementation."*[99] At this hearing six witnesses representing federal agencies, private firms, academia, and an internationally recognized environmental organization offered perspectives on U.S. involvement in the Agreement.[100] With one exception, witnesses voiced support for the Agreement and draft legislation, by claiming that U.S. acceptance of the Agreement offered greater legal certainty for U.S. energy interests in the Gulf of Mexico. The one exception was Mr. Manuel, Sierra Club, arguing that the Agreement was not needed due to the backlog of U.S. leases already in effect in the Gulf of Mexico.[101] Witnesses asserted varying perspectives on the Agreement, based on one or more of the following considerations:

- The Agreement permits, for the first time, firms on the U.S. side of the border to cooperate with Mexico's national oil company, Petróleos Mexicanos (PEMEX) on joint exploration and development projects.[102]
- The Agreement allows more numerous options for U.S. oil and natural gas companies to invest in and to operate in the Gulf of Mexico, creating jobs and enhancing U.S. energy security.[103]
- Lacking specifics about safety and environmental protection, it remains unclear whether the Agreement is compatible with U.S. interests in fishing and tourism in the Gulf of Mexico.[104]

Of the witnesses testifying in favor of legislative review and acceptance of the Agreement, each cited clarifying U.S.-Mexico relations with respect to governing the transboundary area was needed for safe and responsible energy development to commence. In contrast to the testimony of these witnesses, the Sierra Club witness expressed skepticism that swift U.S. acceptance was needed "given that the oil and gas industry is sitting on a large number of inactive leases in federal waters, proving accelerated leasing in the Gulf of Mexico to be unnecessary."[105]

Following these hearings, legislation (S. 812, H.R. 1613) was introduced in both chambers on April 25, 2013. This legislation would approve and implement the Agreement taking slightly differing approaches.[106]

Senate Committee on Energy and Natural Resources

On October 1, 2013, the Senate Committee on Energy and Natural Resources held a legislative hearing on S. 812 and H.R. 1613, as part of examining the proper federal management role relevant to transboundary hydrocarbon reservoirs, and for other purposes. Government witnesses[107] offered testimony consistent with support for implementing the Agreement. Private sector witnesses offered testimony expressing opposing views: industry supporting the implementing legislation and environmental groups expressing objections.[108] The following highlights describe hearing testimony:

- Without the Agreement, firms on both sides of the border will likely not explore and develop deepwater projects of interest to both countries.[109]

- The Agreement allows for more legal certainty for all parties with a stake in planning offshore development scenarios. Many perceive this added certainty as creating a more favorable business atmosphere for U.S. oil and natural gas companies seeking to finance operations in the Gulf of Mexico.[110]
- Lacking detailed provisions related to safety and environmental protection in the Agreement, lifting the current moratorium is premature and raises concerns about pollution events including increased Green House Gas (GHG) emissions and oil spills that could jeopardize U.S. fishing, tourism and other interests in the Gulf of Mexico and elsewhere.[111]

The timing of this hearing and public admission to the hearing were affected by the Senate experiencing the first day of the federal government shutdown.[112] After this hearing the Senate Committee on Energy and Natural Resources discharged S. 812 by unanimous consent. On October 12, 2013, the Senate passed S. 812, without amendment, by unanimous consent.

End Notes

[1] See *Treaty to Resolve the International Boundary*, signed on November 23, 1970; *Treaty on Maritime Boundaries between the United Mexican States and the United States of America*, signed on May 4, 1978; and *Treaty between the Government of the United Mexican States and the Government of the United States of America on the Continental Shelf*, signed on June 9, 2000.

[2] For legal jurisdictions related to ocean energy development, see CRS Report RL33404, *Offshore Oil and Gas Development: Legal Framework*, by Adam Vann.

[3] Under the U.S.-Mexico Transboundary Hydrocarbons Agreement, both countries might proceed with deepwater development via "unitization," a model commonly used for federally regulated drilling in the U.S. Gulf of Mexico. A framework (specifically to support unitization as a model for development, which is explained in a basic fashion in the next section) is widely recognized as necessary for offshore exploration and production to occur.

[4] For details about developments involving China, see CRS Report R42784, *Maritime Territorial and Exclusive Economic Zone (EEZ) Disputes Involving China: Issues for Congress*, by Ronald O'Rourke. For details about developments involving multinational interests in the Arctic, see CRS Report R41153, *Changes in the Arctic: Background and Issues for Congress*, coordinated by Ronald O'Rourke.

[5] Department of State, *Summary of the U.S.-Mexico Transboundary Hydrocarbons Agreement* (July 30, 2012). This summary can be found at http://www.state.gov/r/pa/prs/ps/2012/02/184235.htm.

[6] For a discussion of conditions in Mexico, see CRS Report R42917, *Mexico's Peña Nieto Administration: Priorities and Key Issues in U.S.-Mexican Relations*, by Clare Ribando Seelke.

[7] "Mexico's Congress Could Get Mexico Energy Reform Package Soon, Official Says," *Latin American Herald Tribune*, August 14, 2013. Full article available at http://www.laht.com/ article.asp?ArticleId=812412&CategoryId=14091.

[8] Bureau of Safety and Environmental Enforcement (BSEE, pronounced "Bessy"), is responsible for oversight and enforcement, field operations, inspections, workforce safety, and decommissioning. For analysis of these topics as they relate to recent reforms, see CRS Report R42942, *Deepwater Horizon Oil Spill: Recent Activities and Ongoing Developments*, by Jonathan L. Ramseur and Curry L. Hagerty.

[9] For findings of the cumulative effects of multiple management changes within the DOI bureaus responsible for offshore energy production, see GAO-13-283 *High-Risk Series* (February 14, 2013). This report outlines management challenges related to drilling programs. It is updated every two years, at the start of each new Congress. See also *Department of the Interior: Major Management Challenges*, GAO-11-42T (March 1, 2011).

[10] U.S. Department of State, "Remarks by Secretary of State Hillary Rodham Clinton at the Signing of the U.S.-Mexico Transboundary Agreement," press release, February 20, 2012.

[11] The main tension expressed by supporters and opponents of H.R. 1613, as reported by the House Committee on Natural Resources, involved provisions to exempt actions taken by public companies in accordance with the transboundary hydrocarbon agreement from requirements under Section 1504 of the Dodd-Frank Act and the Securities and Exchange Commission's Natural Resource Extraction Disclosure Rule. For arguments in favor of these provisions, see H.Rept. 113-101, and for counterarguments, see "Statement of Administration Policy on H.R. 1613" (June 25, 2013), at http://www.whitehouse.gov/sites/ default/files/omb/legislative/sap/113/saphr1613r_20130625.pdf.

[12] As noted in the Statement of Administration Policy on H.R. 1613, the Administration supports implementing legislation, without the inclusion of provisions such as those relating to Section 1504 of the Dodd-Frank Act that arguably would dilute U.S. efforts to increase transparency and accountability.

[13] The U.S. EEZ generally includes territory 200 nautical miles seaward of state waters. See Presidential Proclamation No. 5030, 48 *Federal Register* 10605 (March 14, 1983).

[14] Bureau of Ocean Energy Management (BOEM, rhymes with "*Rome*") is tasked with offshore leasing administration, including developing maps, completing scientific and economic analyses, and issuing leases. BOEM also participates in some international relations missions regarding U.S. ocean energy resources.

[15] See Five-Year OCS Oil and Gas Leasing Program 2012-2017. This program was approved on August 27, 2012, and is anticipated to be in place through 2017. Each program is mandated by the Outer Continental Shelf Lands Act (43 U.S.C. §1344) to be "a schedule of proposed lease sales indicating, as precisely as possible, the size, timing, and location of leasing activity which ... will best meet national energy needs."

[16] 43 U.S.C. §1337(p). For more information about deployment of renewable energy projects, see http://www.boem.gov/Renewable-Energy-Program/Smart-from-the-Start/Index.aspx.

[17] After 1953 the federal land tenure system reflected a federal grid system beginning seaward of state submerged land tenure systems. Starting in1983 this grid system recognized the U.S. EEZ.

[18] For the purposes of this report, the state and federal waters of the Gulf of Mexico are defined as follows: Florida waters extend 9 nautical miles (10.4 statute miles) from shore; Louisiana, Mississippi, and Alabama state waters extend 3 nautical miles (or 3.5 statute miles) from shore; and Texas state waters extend 9 nautical miles (10.4 statute miles) from shore. For a comprehensive analysis of coastal and marine uses in the western Gulf of Mexico, see *2012-2017 Western Planning Area/Central Planning Area Multisale Environmental Impact Statement (EIS)*, BOEM, available at http://www.boem.gov/uploadedFiles/BOEM/ Environmental_Stewardship/Environmental_Assessment/NEPA/BOEM-2012-019_v3.pdf.

[19] Statistics about annual energy supplies and annual receipts from bonus bids, rentals, and royalties are published through numerous sources. The statistics in this report are derived

from the Office of Natural Resources Revenue within DOI, available at
http://www.ONRR.gov.

[20] For ocean energy revenue statistics, see http://www.ONRR.gov. FY2012 federal offshore
reported revenues were $6.9 billion; FY2011, $6.5 billion; and FY2010, $5.3 billion.

[21] See DOI *FY2014 Congressional Budget Justification*, Bureau of Ocean Energy Management
(BOEM), p. 12. DOI bases this statement on assumptions about bonus payments and other
predicted revenue streams for rentals and taxes deriving from operations in the
transboundary area cited in the Agreement. Estimates of federal budget effects vary widely.
For example, a recent estimate by the Congressional Budget Office (CBO) provided as part
of analysis of a specific bill to implement the Agreement (H.R. 1613) concluded that
approving and implementing the Agreement in that instance would increase federal receipts
by $25 million from 2014 through 2023.

[22] International customary law provides frameworks for governance of some but not all areas and
activities beyond national jurisdictions such as a nation's EEZ. One widely recognized
framework is the United Nations Convention of the Law of the Sea (UNCLOS), a
multilateral treaty with which the United States participates as a non-party. While not
directly applicable to U.S-Mexico bilateral compacts in the Gulf of Mexico, Article 76 of
UNCLOS has provided a process for claiming extended continental shelf (ECS) areas
resulting in territorial claims reaching 350 nautical miles from a country's coastal areas.

[23] Each of these issues is discussed in the section of this report entitled "Pending Legislation."

[24] Joint commitments listed in the Agreement involve goals for the safe and equitable exploitation
of transboundary reservoirs. These commitments are intended to unfold over many years
through further negotiations aimed at facilitating more specific approaches to such issues as
standards for operations and environmental review. Until the Agreement is accepted, the
timeline for implementation remains unclear. Numerous federal regulators might be
involved in activities covered by the Agreement. Operational safety and revenue obligations
related to any future oil and gas leases have already been delegated to BOEM. See CRS
Report R42599, *Department of the Interior (DOI) Reorganization of Ocean Energy
Programs*, by Curry L. Hagerty.

[25] The Submerged Lands Act (SLA), 43 U.S.C. §§1301 et seq. Consistent with SLA, most federal
obligations are defined relative to the jurisdictional bounds of state and federal waters.

[26] The Outer Continental Shelf Lands Act of 1953 (OCSLA), 43 U.S.C. §§1331 et seq. Consistent
with OCSLA, federal mandatory and discretionary responsibilities are defined for energy
resource management and revenue management in areas beyond state waters referred to as
the Outer Continental Shelf (OCS).

[27] U.S. commitments relative to managing ocean energy resources in international waters involve
various treaties. Separate from the U.S.-Mexico bilateral treaties discussed above, the
United States is party to four prominent ocean governance treaties adopted in 1958:
Convention on the Territorial Sea and the Contiguous Zone, Convention on the High Seas,
Convention on the Continental Shelf, and Convention on Fishing and Conservation of the
Living Resources of the High Seas.

[28] To help understand the role of the House of Representatives with respect to review of this
Agreement, it is important to clarify that the Agreement has not been submitted to the
Senate as a treaty. Under the U.S. system, a legally binding international agreement can take
different forms. Unlike agreements taking the form of a treaty (that would enter into force if
approved by a two-thirds majority of the Senate and subsequently ratified by the President),
this Agreement was negotiated and signed by the executive branch as a non-treaty. In the
case of a non-treaty, to be legally binding, it must either be authorized by a statute passed
by Congress ("congressional executive agreements") or a prior treaty approved by the
Senate, except when it concerns matters falling under the exclusive constitutional authority
of the President ("sole executive agreements"). For further discussion, see CRS Report
RL32528, *International Law and Agreements: Their Effect upon U.S. Law*, by Michael John
Garcia.

[29] H.R. 1613 was referred to three committees: Committee on Natural Resources; Committee on Foreign Affairs and Committee on Financial Services. On June 6, 2013, the Committees on Foreign Affairs and Financial Services discharged the bill.

[30] In addition, H.R. 1613 offers placeholders for implementing Agreements with four other countries: Canada, Russia, the Bahamas, and Bermuda. Although placeholders are sometimes included in bills that are introduced, they have rarely been enacted as law.

[31] Securities Exchange Act of 1934, 157 U.S.C. 78m(q).This section of the bill is summarized by Gary Shorter, CRS Specialist in Financial Economics.

[32] CRS Report R41350, *The Dodd-Frank Wall Street Reform and Consumer Protection Act: Issues and Summary*, coordinated by Baird Webel.

[33] In general, the American Petroleum Institute (API) and other business groups have resisted implementation of Section 1504 of the Dodd-Frank Act. This resistance has been demonstrated by challenging SEC's new rule requiring publicly traded U.S. oil and gas companies to report information about projects that potentially could benefit their overseas national oil companies.

[34] Descriptions of SEC obligations were authored by Gary Shorter, CRS Specialist in Financial Economics.

[35] See DOI FY2014 Budget Justifications, "Budget Highlights," p. 23. See also BOEM Office of Congressional Affairs written communication to CRS, May 16, 2013. The budget justification refers to draft legislation offered by the Administration to the House and the Senate as follows:

The Secretary is authorized to take actions necessary to implement the terms of the Agreement between the United States of America and the United Mexican States Concerning Transboundary Hydrocarbon Reservoirs in the Gulf of Mexico, which is hereby approved, including: to approve unitization agreements and related arrangements for the exploration of, and development or production of oil or gas from, transboundary reservoirs and geological structures; to disclose as necessary under such an Agreement information related to the exploration, development, and production of a transboundary reservoir or geological structure that may be considered confidential, privileged, or proprietary information under law; and to accept and take action not inconsistent with an expert determination under such an Agreement.

[36] 157 U.S.C. 78m(q). For a discussion of this theme, see http://thehill.com/blogs/e2-wire/e2-wire/296235-house-gop-moves-to-shield-oil-companies-from-disclosure-rules# ixzz2RyR0jqGZ.

[37] The *Deepwater* Horizon events resulted in 11 worker fatalities, a massive oil release, and a national response effort in the Gulf of Mexico led by the federal government. Based on estimates from the U.S. Geological Survey, the oil spill was the largest in U.S. waters.

[38] 76 *Federal Register* 64432 (October 18, 2011). BSEE revised 30 CFR Chapter II. For a status report, see CRS Report R42942, *Deepwater Horizon Oil Spill: Recent Activities and Ongoing Developments*, by Jonathan L. Ramseur and Curry L. Hagerty.

[39] Gene L. Dodaro, U.S. Comptroller General, testimony before the House Committee on Oversight and Government Reform, February 17, 2011; Committee on Appropriations, Subcommittee on Interior, Hearing March 17, 2011. GAO-13-283 *High-Risk Series* (February 14, 2013). This GAO report is updated at the start of each new Congress.

[40] On November 28, 2012, BOEM offered offshore oil and gas development rights beyond the U.S. EEZ and near the marine boundary area with Mexico as part of the public lease sale referred to as Sale 229. Prior to U.S. leasing activities near the U.S.-Mexico continental shelf boundary, BOEM issued the following statement: "Within 30 days following the approval of the Agreement between the United States of America and the United Mexican States Concerning Transboundary Hydrocarbon Reservoirs in the Gulf of Mexico or by May 31, 2013, whichever occurs first, the Secretary of the Interior will determine whether it is in the best interest of the United States either to open bids for boundary area blocks or to return the bids unopened." The sale drew 131 bids on 116 ocean tracts from 13 companies.

Ocean tracts offered at the sale were located from just beyond Texas state waters to acreage beyond the U.S. EEZ. A previous Western Gulf lease sale (Sale 218 conducted in December 2011) offered acreage in this general area, attracting 241 bids on 191 ocean tracts from 20 companies. For details about the most recent sale, see http://www.boem.gov/Oil-and-Gas-Energy-Program/Leasing/Regional-Leasing/Gulf-of-Mexico-Region/Lease-Sales/229/index.aspx.

[41] This sale entailed 3,864 tracts from 9 to more than 250 miles off the U.S. coast, in water depths ranging from 16 to more than 10,975 feet. BOEM estimated this lease sale could result in the production of 116 million to 200 million barrels of oil and 538 billion to 938 billion cubic feet of natural gas. Following this sale, bids are going through an evaluation process within BOEM to ensure the public receives fair market value before a lease is awarded. Sale statistics for Sale 233 can be found at http://www.boem.gov/Sale-233.

[42] U.S. Department of State, "Mexico, Pollution: Marine Environment, Agreement signed July 24, 1980," TIAS, 10021.

[43] U.S. Coast Guard, "Mexus Plan, The Joint Contingency Plan Between the United Mexican States and the United States of America Regarding Pollution of the Marine Environment by Discharges of Hydrocarbons and Other Hazardous Substance," February 25, 2000. Furthermore, *National Commission on the BP Deepwater Horizon Oil Spill and Offshore Drilling* January 2011, reports that Mexico already conducts safety drills in the Gulf of Mexico and that it is in the U.S. national interest to engage in a common, rigorous system of regulatory oversight to cooperate on containment and response strategies in case of a spill. See *Deepwater, The Gulf Oil Disaster and the Future of Offshore Drilling*, Report to the President, p. 254 and p. 300, at http://www.oilspillcommission.gov/sites/default/files/documents/DEEPWATER_ReporttothePresident_FINAL.pdf.

[44] In these areas, referred to as "gaps," national marine boundaries have not been fully defined. The Western Gap is the polygon located near the Mexican coast of Tamaulipas and the U.S. coast of Houston, TX. The Eastern Gap is the polygon located near the Mexican coast of Yucatan, the U.S. coast of New Orleans, LA, and the coast of Cuba. A discussion of the Eastern Gap is beyond the scope of this report. The Western Gap is depicted in **Figure 6**.

[45] According to BOEM, the division of the Western Gap allocates 1,507,840 acres or 38% to the United States and 2,624,000 acres or 62% to Mexico.

[46] See H.Rept. 113-101, Part 1, p. 4. "Currently, there are 67 active lease blocks held by nine companies on the U.S. portion of the Western Gap, meaning roughly 20% of the available acreage in the Western Gap area is under lease." For a discussion of U.S. leasing activities in the western Gulf of Mexico beyond the U.S. EEZ and potentially subject to the provisions of international agreements, see *U.S. Accession to U.N. Convention on the Law of the Sea Unnecessary to Develop Oil and Gas Resources, Backgrounder No. 2668*, by Steven Groves, May 14, 2012, p. 9.

[47] Analysis of the Eastern Gap area is beyond the scope of this report. For more information about the Eastern Gap and how the U.S.-Mexican boundaries for this area were drawn, see *GPS World* (May, 2001) available at http://www.ngs.noaa.gov/CORS/Articles/solgps.pdf.

[48] U.S. Department of State, *Summary of the U.S.–Mexico Transboundary Hydrocarbons Agreement*, July 30, 2012, http://www.state.gov/r/pa/prs/ps/2012/02/184235.htm. For the purpose of this report, all treaties are referred to by the year the treaty is signed. Accordingly, this treaty is the "1970 Treaty." In November 1970, the two nations established their maritime boundaries in the Gulf of Mexico; the treaty entered into force on April 18, 1972.

[49] Transboundary reservoirs straddle marine areas between government (nations or U.S. coastal states). Unitization is one approach to determining the recovery of oil from these areas. This concept is discussed throughout this report and is defined in the text box on p. 19.

[50] For the full set of remarks at the signing of the U.S.-Mexico Transboundary Agreement, Los Cabos, Mexico, February 20, 2012, see http://www.state.gov/secretary/rm/2012/02/184236.htm.

[51] This section does not provide a comprehensive legal examination of the Agreement's contents and does not offer an in-depth analysis of U.S. interests in various provisions. A variety of topics addressed in other CRS reports analyze policy perspectives surrounding U.S. interests in the Agreement: peacetime military engagement; fisheries enforcement, search and rescue, drug interdiction, trade, investment and marine pollution law enforcement. These topics are distinct in many ways from topics surrounding U.S. interests in managing ocean energy resources in U.S. waters. For more information on these aspects of U.S.-Mexico relations, see CRS Report R42917, *Mexico's Peña Nieto Administration: Priorities and Key Issues in U.S.-Mexican Relations*, by Clare Ribando Seelke; CRS Report R41349, *U.S.-Mexican Security Cooperation: The Mérida Initiative and Beyond*, by Clare Ribando Seelke and Kristin Finklea; and CRS Report R42965, NAFTA at 20: *Overview and Trade Effects*, by M. Angeles Villarreal and Ian F. Fergusson.

[52] Article 1 provides that the Agreement applies to areas extending "across the Delimitation Line" This line begins beyond 9 nautical miles from the coastline of Texas and ends 550 miles to the east, at the point to the west of the Eastern Gap.

[53] Article 2 provides definitions for 24 terms, starting with "Confidential Data" and ending with "Unit Operating Agreement."

[54] Article 3 states that nothing in the Agreement "shall be interpreted as affecting the sovereign rights and the jurisdiction which each Party has under international law ..."

[55] Article 4 establishes requirements for consultations "on exploration and exploitation activities" carried out within certain areas surrounding the Delimitation Line.

[56] Article 5 outlines a multi-step process for reaching a determination on the existence of a Transboundary Reservoir. This determination entails deadlines for consultations and submissions to the "Joint Commission" as defined elsewhere in the Agreement.

[57] Article 6 details the components of a Unitization Agreement, including requirements to measure production; procedures for ensuring accurate payments of royalties and other proceeds; and safety and environmental measures to be taken under the national laws of each party.

[58] Article 7 addresses management guidelines prior to the formation of a transboundary unit.

[59] Articles 8 and 9 provide for determining and redetermining allocation of production.

[60] Article 10 reads as follows: "The Executive Agencies shall ensure that a unit operator for a Transboundary Unit is designated by agreement between the Licensees. The designation or change of the unit operator shall be subject to the approval of the Executive Agencies. The unit operator will act on behalf of the Licensees."

[61] Articles 11 and 12 provide general guidelines addressing operational aspects of a project to facilitate cooperation between relevant parties.

[62] Article 13 provides the following: "Income arising from the Exploitation of Transboundary Reservoirs shall be taxed in accordance with the legislation of the United Mexican States and the United States of America respectively, as well as the Convention between the Government of the United States of America and the Government of the United Mexican States for the Avoidance of Double Taxation and the Prevention of Fiscal Evasion with respect to Taxes on Income and Capital, signed on September 18th, 1992, as amended (and as may be amended in the future), or any Convention superseding that Convention as the Parties may enter into in the future."

[63] Article 14 is more detailed than most other provisions in the Agreement. It refers to powers vested in the Joint Commission for resolving differences concerning the allocation of production pursuant to Articles 8 and 9. It sets deadlines for the Joint Commission to act and provides alternatives for resolving disputes.

[64] Articles 15, 16 and 17 provide broad guidelines for consultations, mediation, expert determination and arbitration. These guidelines include multiple references to deadlines and to terms defined elsewhere in the Agreement.

[65] Articles 18 and 19 generally reference "applicable national law" as a basis of joint inspections in the area.

[66] Articles 20, 21, 22, and 23 provide details about amending, terminating and bringing this Agreement into force.

[67] Article 24 reads as follows: "Upon entry into force of this Agreement, the period of any moratorium on the authorization or permitting of petroleum or natural gas drilling or exploration of the continental shelf within the boundary "Area" as established by Article 4, paragraph 1, of the 2000 Treaty on the Continental Shelf and extended by any subsequent exchanges of notes shall be terminated."

[68] Article 25 asserts that "nothing in this Agreement shall affect the rights and obligations of the Parties with respect to other international agreements to which they are both party."

[69] On June 23, 2010, a Joint Statement was adopted by President Obama and then-President Calderon at the conclusion of then-President Calderon's State Visit to Washington on May 19, 2010. For the full set of remarks, see http://www.whitehouse.gov/the-press-office/joint-statement-president-barack-obama-and-president-felipe-calder-n. See also *Joint Statement by President Barack Obama, President Felipe Calderon of Mexico, and Prime Minister Stephen Harper of Canada on Climate Change and Clean Energy* (August 10, 2009).

[70] For the full set of remarks at the signing of the U.S.-Mexico Transboundary Agreement, Los Cabos, Mexico, February 20, 2012, see http://www.state.gov/secretary/rm/2012/02/184236.htm.

[71] Information used for this section was obtained from the U.S. Department of State Fact Sheet dated February 20, 2012, and found at http://www.state.gov/r/pa/prs/ps/2012/02/184235.htm.

[72] See joint statement adopted by Presidents Obama and Calderon, Washington, DC, May 19, 2010.

[73] Concurrent with regulating operations in the Gulf of Mexico, DOI is assessing energy resource potential off the coast of the Mid- and South Atlantic and off the coasts of California and Alaska, including in the Chukchi and Beaufort Seas. For a comprehensive statement of current federal policies toward offshore oil and gas development, see 77 *Federal Register* 40080 (July 6, 2012).

[74] For a full CBO report on H.R. 1613, see http://www.cbo.gov/sites/default/files/cbofiles/attachments/hr1613.pdf.

[75] For information about the lease sales referred to in the CBO score see Five-Year Outer Continental Shelf (OCS) Oil and Gas Leasing Program for 2012–2017, 77 *Federal Register* 40080 (July 6, 2012).

[76] Transboundary Agreement, Articles 2, 6, 7, 8, 9, 10, 11, 12, 18, 22, 23. See also S.Rept. 112-43, *Oil Mexico, and the Transboundary Agreement*, Senate Committee on Foreign Relations (December 21, 2012). See also 30 CFR 250 Subpart M. See http://www.bsee.gov/Exploration-and-Production/Unitization/Unitization.aspx.

[77] A "vertical access" facility is a system comprising a floating host located over a drilling location with the floating host comprising drilling functions. More information on this facility can be found at http://www.shell.com.

[78] In the United States, the 110th Congress allowed the annual congressional moratoriums included in DOI appropriations acts to expire on September 30, 2008, and did not extend these congressional bans on oil and gas leasing activities (P.L. 110-329). Legislation related to domestic moratoriums has been driven by support for promoting domestic energy production to improve energy security, and increasing offshore receipts and disbursements.

[79] See statement of Nicolette Nye, spokeswoman for National Ocean Industries Association (NOIA) in "U.S.-Mexico transboundary Agreement mired in Congress," January 8, 2013, at http://www.eenews.net/gw/sample/print/3. See statement of Greenpeace, "Transboundary Agreement Spells Disaster for the Gulf," February 22, 2012.

[80] In April 2009, the United States and Mexico touched on this and other themes as part of launching a comprehensive effort—the Bilateral Framework on Clean Energy and Climate Change—to explore ways to further develop the potential of an energy relationship. With its focus on renewable energy, energy efficiency, jobs and technology development, the

Bilateral Framework has supported work on common standards, closer integration of electricity grids and other development goals in border regions.

[81] See Gulf of Mexico Energy Security Act of 2006 (GOMESA, P.L. 109-432).

[82] The LWCF is a trust fund that accumulates $900 million at the end of each fiscal year. While most of the $900 million is derived from offshore revenues, additional monies have been provided by surplus property sales, and DOI fees otherwise collected from public lands. The National Historic Preservation Act of 1966 establishes the Historic Preservation Fund, made up annually of monies intended for matching grants to the states and to the National Trust for Historic Preservation. These funds are not administered as typical "trust funds." Both consist of monies that cannot be spent unless appropriated by Congress. From FY1965 through FY2012, less than half the accumulated funds in the LWCF have been appropriated. For more information, see CRS Report RL33531, *Land and Water Conservation Fund: Overview, Funding History, and Issues*, by Carol Hardy Vincent.

[83] U.S. Government Accountability Office, *Border Security: Additional Actions Needed to Better Ensure a Coordinated Federal Response to Illegal Activity on Federal Lands*, GAO-11-177, November 2010, pp. 9-10.

[84] The Bureau of Safety and Environmental Enforcement (BSEE, pronounced "Bessy") is tasked with DOI oversight and enforcement for offshore field operations, inspections, workforce safety, and decommissioning. Other than BSEE authorities pursuant to OCSLA, BSEE responsibilities are governed by the National Environmental Policy Act of 1969 (NEPA P.L. 91-190; 42 U.S.C. §§ 4321-4347 and implementing regulations 40 C.F.R. Part 1500.

[85] For more information on compliance with NEPA in relation to U.S. border programs, see CBP, "SBI Environmental Documents," http://www.cbp.gov/xp/cgov/border_security/otia/ sbi_news/sbi_enviro_docs/. A related issue is the authority, and litigation challenging the authority, related to waivers from environmental protection statutes.

[86] For information on issues related to border barriers, see CRS Report R42138, *Border Security: Immigration Enforcement Between Ports of Entry*, by Marc R. Rosenblum.

[87] In the absence of physical development, other than company disclosures and agency lease tenure records, there is little to indicate the role these leases play in the offshore ocean energy program. GAO, *Oil and Gas Leasing: Interior Could Do More to Encourage Diligent Development*, GAO-09-74 (Washington, D.C.: Oct. 3, 2008). See also *Oil and Gas Lease Utilization, Onshore and Offshore*, Updated Report to the President DOI (May 2012).

[88] In theory, important tax implications can stem from how taxpayers with OCS leases determine their value. Specifically, the character of any losses or gains (e.g., capital asset or ordinary income, carried interest) associated with OCS leases could, in theory, be a factor for some firms maintaining an increasing number of undeveloped tracts.

[89] The offshore drilling debate is a combination of several discrete debates about oil and gas leasing activity in federal and international waters. Congress addresses multiple issues related to access (state-federal consultations about state revenue sharing, adequacy of environmental reviews, timetables for drilling permitting, operational safety, federal receipts and disbursements to federal programs, research).

[90] See, for example, Greenpeace, *Transboundary Agreement Spells Disaster for the Gulf*, February 22, 2012.

[91] H.Rept. 113-101, including Dissenting Views.

[92] For a comprehensive discussion of U.S.-Mexican relations see CRS Report R42917, *Mexico's Peña Nieto Administration: Priorities and Key Issues in U.S.-Mexican Relations*, by Clare Ribando Seelke.

[93] This Agreement has been characterized as very technical in nature, as compared to earlier U.S.-Mexico compacts related to governance of acreage in western Gulf of Mexico. For a discussion detailing the technical aspects of the Agreement see *U.S.-Mexico Agreement on Transboundary Hydrocarbon Reservoirs in the Gulf of Mexico: A Blueprint for Progress or a Recipe for Conflict?* by Jorge A Vargas, (San Diego International Law Journal Fall, 2012).

94 See   http://foreignaffairs.house.gov/hearing/subcommittee-hearing-us-energy-security
   enhancing-partnerships-mexico-and-canada.

95 Witnesses included Duncan Wood, Ph.D., Director, Mexico Institute, The Wilson Center;
   Daniel R. Simmons, Director of Regulatory and State Affairs, Institute for Energy
   Research; Kyle Isakower, Vice President, Regulatory and Economic Policy, American
   Petroleum Institute; Michael A. Levi, Ph.D., Senior Fellow for Energy and the
   Environment, and Director of the Program on Energy Security and Climate Change,
   Council on Foreign Relations. No Administration witness was on the panel.

96 Testimony of Duncan Wood.

97 Testimony of Kyle Isakower.

98 Testimony of Michael Levi.

99 See   http://foreignaffairs.house.gov/hearing/subcommittee-hearing-us-energy-security-enhan
   cing-partnerships-mexico-and-canada.

100 Witnesses included Tommy Beaudreau, Acting Assistant Secretary for Land and Minerals
    Management U.S. Department of the Interior (DOI); Ambassador Carlos Pascual, Special
    Envoy and Coordinator for International Energy Affairs U.S. Department of State (DOS);
    Erik Milito, American Petroleum Institute; Daniel R. Simmons, Institute for Energy
    Research; Steven Groves, Heritage Foundation; and, Athan Manuel, Sierra Club.

101 Sierra   Club   statement   is   found   at   http://naturalresources.house.gov/uploadedfiles/
    manueltestimony04-25-13.pdf.

102 This point was made by both Mr. Beaudreau (DOI) and Ambassador Pascual (DOS). For the
    complete written testimony of both witnesses see http://naturalresources.house.gov/
    uploadedfiles/beaudreautestimony04-25-13.pdf   and   http://naturalresources.house.gov/
    uploadedfiles/pascualtestimony04-25-13.pdf.

103 This point was made by both Mr. Milito and Mr. Groves. For the complete written testimony
    of both witnesses see http://naturalresources.house.gov/uploadedfiles/militotestimony04-25-
    13.pdf and http://naturalresources.house.gov/uploadedfiles/grovestestimony04-25-13.pdf.

104 This point was made by Mr. Manuel. For the complete Sierra Club statement see
    http://naturalresources.house.gov/uploadedfiles/manueltestimony04-25-13.pdf.

105 See Sierra Club written testimony, p. 3. For further information on offshore acreage leased but
    not producing see *Oil and Gas Lease Utilization – Onshore and Offshore*, Report to the
    President, U.S. Department of the Interior (March, 2011) found at http://www.doi.gov/
    news/pressreleases/loader.cfm?csModule=security/getfile&pageid=239255.

106 These bills are summarized in the section of this report entitled "Pending Legislation."

107 Ambassador Carlos Pascual, Special Envoy and Coordinator, International Energy Affairs,
    U.S. Department of State and Tommy P. Beaudreau, Acting Assistant Secretary, Land and
    Minerals Management, DOI.

108 Ms. Jacqueline Savitz, Vice President, U.S. Oceans, Oceana expressed opposition to both
    bills; Mr. Erik Milito, Director, Upstream and Industry Operations, expressed American
    Petroleum Institute support for the legislation.

109 This point was made by Mr. Beaudreau (DOI) and Ambassador Pascual (DOS) and Mr.
    Milito. For the complete written testimony of these witnesses see http://www.energy.senate.
    gov/public/index.cfm/2013/10/full-committee-hearing-to-consider-s-812-and-h-r-1613.

110 This point was made by both government and industry witnesses.

111 This point was made by Ms. Savitz. For the complete Oceana statement see
    http://www.energy.senate.gov/public/index.cfm/files/serve?File_id=4acfb140-c30a-4baf-
    9513-710733d3c945.

112 CRS Report RL34680, *Shutdown of the Federal Government: Causes, Processes, and Effects*,
    coordinated by Clinton T. Brass.

In: U.S.-Mexico Transboundary Hydrocarbons ...   ISBN: 978-1-63117-307-3
Editor: Hugh Bruner   © 2014 Nova Science Publishers, Inc.

Chapter 2

OIL, MEXICO, AND THE TRANSBOUNDARY AGREEMENT[*]

Minority Staff of the Senate Committee on Foreign Relations

LETTER OF TRANSMITTAL

United States Senate,
Committee On Foreign Relations,
Washington, DC, December 21, 2012

Dear Colleagues: Energy security is a vital issue for United States foreign policy and economic growth. Increases in U.S. domestic oil production are helping relieve our import dependence, yet our nation will rely on oil imports for decades to come. Strengthening trade with reliable, friendly neighbors Canada and Mexico would make a valuable contribution to our future.

I directed Senate Foreign Relations Committee Senior Staff Members Neil Brown and Carl Meacham to assess opportunities for enhancing the U.S.-Mexico oil and natural gas relationship. Mexico is a reliable trading partner. Yet it continues to struggle to maintain and increase its domestic oil production. Falling quantities of Mexican heavy oil available for U.S. Gulf

---

[*] This report was released by the Senate Foreign Relations Committee on December 21, 2012.

Coast refineries have actually helped lead to increases in Middle Eastern imports to the U.S. even as our total imports have fallen.

Congress needs to understand the obstacles—and opportunities— ahead in Mexico's oil production. Put bluntly, we know that we can rely on Mexico as a trading partner, but we do not know the quantity or the quality of oil to expect it to be able to export in the years ahead.

Given domestic political sensitivities about oil within Mexico, the bilateral relationship on this topic has struggled. Yet, the newly elected President of Mexico has signaled a desire to work together on energy issues, and the largest opposition political party joins in that call.

I urge my colleagues, and the Obama administration, to seize today's opportunity. My staff identified specific areas in shale gas, safety enhancement, transparency, and security that represent near-term opportunities for bilateral gain.

I strongly encourage the Obama administration to send the U.S.- Mexico Transboundary Agreement, signed in February of this year, to Congress and urge my colleagues to pass the agreement. The Transboundary Agreement is good for energy security, good for the environment, good for U.S. commercial interests, and, most critically, can open the door to bilateral engagement on shared energy interests.

This report provides useful insight on the need and prospects for domestic oil sector reforms in Mexico and important recommendations for the U.S. government to take in order to strengthen U.S.- Mexico energy cooperation. I hope that you find this report by Mr. Brown and Mr. Meacham helpful and look forward to working with you on these issues.

Sincerely,
Richard G. Lugar,
Ranking Member.

OVERSIGHT STUDY

Senator Richard G. Lugar, Ranking Member of the Senate Foreign Relations Committee, requested senior professional staff members to review opportunities for enhanced U.S.-Mexico engagement on oil and gas issues including the U.S.-Mexico Transboundary Agreement, which requires Congressional action to take effect.

As part of that review, members of Senator Lugar's staff traveled to Mexico City in October 2012 to meet with then President-elect Enrique Peña Nieto's transition team and leaders from the Mexican Congress, PEMEX, the Mexican energy regulator Comisión Nacional de Hidrocarburos, U.S. industry, academic specialists, and U.S. officials at Embassy Mexico City.[1] This report contains their public findings and recommendations.

Congressional attention to the Mexican energy situation is critical for understanding bilateral issues between our countries and for consideration of U.S. energy security.

The United States has a profound interest in economic prosperity and political stability in Mexico, and energy is foundational to both interests. Oil is vital for the Mexican federal budget, underwriting both social programs and law and order, and the oil industry is an important aspect of broader economic activity. Stability and growth, or lack thereof, in Mexico's oil and gas sector can directly impact issues of bilateral concern.

Mexico is also important for U.S. energy security, providing a nearby and politically reliable source for oil imports. Recently overtaken by Saudi Arabia, Mexico has been the second largest source of oil imports to the United States, with Canada being the largest.

However, falling Mexican oil production and rising demand led to increases in U.S. imports from the Middle East, and maintaining the current levels of Mexican oil production, let alone achieving rapid growth in production, have a dubious future without reforms.[2] Thorough energy security policy in Washington requires constant assessment of the Mexican oil industry. If Mexico does not reform its domestic energy production situation, the U.S. cannot rely on current levels of imports.

The SFRC staff's examination was timely because of recent Mexican elections for President and Congress. The newly elected Mexican President, Enrique Peña Nieto, campaigned promising to institute energy reforms and has continued that theme since taking office. Reform, or lack thereof, negotiated between the Mexican President and Congress will have consequences for the U.S. energy portfolio and commercial interests.

The examination is also timely because the United States Congress is expected to review and act on the U.S.-Mexico Transboundary Agreement signed in February 2012, which was ratified in Mexico with a great deal of fanfare and also has support of major international oil companies operating in the United States.

MEXICAN OIL AND GAS: CRITICAL FOR MEXICO'S PROSPERITY, IN CRITICAL NEED OF REFORM

Mexican hydrocarbon resources belong to the Mexican people. Popular enthusiasm and national pride is attached to those resources, and many Mexicans directly depend on the existing oil industry for their livelihood and business interests. Crossing into the territory of energy sector reform requires political courage on behalf of Mexican politicians. The United States government emphatically recognizes the privileged position of oil in Mexico's politics.

Nonetheless, the United States has direct interests in the future of oil and natural gas in Mexico. Most important among U.S. interests is enhancing the prosperity of the Mexican people. With strong cultural ties and a shared border, the U.S. benefits when Mexico grows. Petroleos Mexicanos (PEMEX) has successfully staved off years of decreasing oil production and discovered deep water resources, but it has not been able to meaningfully increase production beyond its zone of comfort in shallow water. Without reform, Mexico's oil resources will not be developed in a way that translates into a higher quality of life for Mexicans.

Mexico is a reliable supplier of oil to the United States. The question for U.S. policymakers is what volumes Mexico will be able to export in the future. Mexican production dropped by more than a quarter in the last decade, leaving U.S. refiners on the Gulf Coast geared for heavy oil having to look elsewhere. Venezuelan heavy oil production has also collapsed. Canadian heavy crude production is increasing in the oil sands region, but pipeline infrastructure is insufficient. Therefore, in effect, the U.S. has had to increase imports of Middle East crudes in order to make up for shortfalls in Mexico.

Understanding the likely trajectory of reform in Mexico is necessary to appropriately plan for future volumes and types of crude oil traded with the United States, which also will have broader implications for U.S. security and economic growth. Mexican energy reforms will determine to what extent Mexico will be part of future U.S., and North American, energy security.

Progress, but Can It Last? A Snapshot of Mexico's Oil Sector

Mexico has a long history of oil production and has prospects for a bright future as an oil power, but such an outcome is not guaranteed. Mexico sits atop significant amounts of oil estimated at 10.4 billion barrels of proven reserves, but that number could more than double when unconventional and deep offshore reserves are fully proven. The large unconventional Chicontopec area alone is estimated to hold up to 17.7 billion barrels.

Turning Mexico's oil resources into prosperity for the Mexican people is a tremendous challenge for PEMEX, its 100% state-owned national oil company established in 1938 after international oil companies were expelled.[3]

Mexican oil production relies primarily on a few major fields, the largest of which (Cantarell) is in steep decline. Oil production in Mexico peaked in 2003 at about 3.4 million barrels per day (mbd), falling to 2.6 mbd in 2010. That precipitous fall is due primarily to the estimated 75% decline in production from the massive Cantarell field from its peak. In recent years, Cantarell's decline has been compensated for by the Ku-Maloob-Zaap (KMZ) fields; however, many analysts doubt the longevity of current production in those fields.

Large increases in direct and third-party investment in recent years has enabled PEMEX to halt net decreases in production, at least temporarily. Importantly, PEMEX also now reports achieving a 100% replacement rate for reserves, improving prospects for continued production. Increased investment also has led to discoveries of large new deep water resources at Trion, Supremos, and Maximino, achievements of which PEMEX officials are justifiably proud. Several interlocutors credited energy reforms passed in 2008 for enabling those finds by giving PEMEX more flexibility to partner with international companies on a service contract basis, building on the shift to reliance on contracting services to enable investments stretching from the late 1990s.

PEMEX leaders plan to raise production to 2.7 mbd in 2013 and 3 mbd by 2017, requiring up to $38 billion annually in investment. Near term growth is expected to come primarily from Chicontopec, a highly complex unconventional onshore project that is subject of great hope and scorn. Despite years of development and reportedly $5 billion in investment, the project is well behind expectations and currently only 70,000 barrels per day are produced, which puts claims of near-term growth in serious doubt. Over the longer-term PEMEX has set a goal to increase production to 3.3 mbd by 2024. Achieving that goal will require significantly more new production than the difference between the 3.3 mbd goal and today's 2.6 mbd given expected large declines in KMZ.

Field decline emphasizes the urgent need for Mexico to have several new projects in the pipeline in order to maintain and boost production. Skepticism of PEMEX's ability to compensate for declining fields has led to some dire forecasts. The U.S. Energy Information Administration has estimated that Mexico will be a net importer of oil by 2020,[4] thus also raising concerns about impacts on its balance of trade. While not investigated on this StaffDel, that situation highlights the need for more attention to demand management policies and continued reform of fuel subsidies.[5]

Mexico needs a diverse portfolio of future oil projects with staggered capacities over time. PEMEX leaders have identified such a set of oil development projects, including deep offshore and the Chicontopec unconventional area, each of which are complex undertakings with high potential, forming a growth strategy to complement conventional shallow offshore projects and investment in enhanced recovery at previous wells. Some observers point out that privatization of the sector would bring competition and private investment; however, that prospect is so remote as to be non-existent and not under even speculative consideration. Therefore, the question is what PEMEX can achieve on its own or in partnership with international companies.

Most interlocutors are skeptical of PEMEX having the capital or expertise necessary to develop deep offshore fields, and, probably, the unconventional reserves at Chicontopec. Analysts point out that PEMEX took over 15 years and more than 20 wells to discover the most recent deep water finds. Moreover, deep water requires massive investments over many years, and even the world's largest international oil companies (IOCs) partner with one another to generate capital and spread the risk of such investments. PEMEX's capital limitations are further complicated by the company's large debt burden. On the other side, proponents of PEMEX's ability argue that they have gained expertise and dramatically lessened the risks implicit in development.

PEMEX likely could develop a deep offshore project by buying technology and expertise through very generous service contracts with many of the same companies with which the IOCs contract. However, under current capital and management constraints,[6] PEMEX alone is extremely unlikely to have the resources necessary to undertake multiple massive deep offshore developments while also investing in conventional oil production. Moreover, while some technology can be purchased through service contracts, project management expertise to run that type of project is not easily acquired.

Therefore, the decision on whether IOCs should be granted access individually or in partnership with PEMEX to develop oil in Mexico depends on how much oil the Mexican Government wants produced and over what span of time. Interlocutors did not indicate that the expectations of either of the largest political parties or the Mexican public are conducive to the long time horizons it would take for PEMEX under current conditions to fully develop Mexico's oil.

Dealing with this challenge is complicated by the fact that PEMEX is as much a bureau of the government as it is a company. In defiance of conventional business sense (of both private companies and state oil companies), multiple Ministries and a politically- appointed Board of Directors make key decisions, including deciding the amount and direction of investment in exploration and development of future production. It is not clear that all board members put the interests of the company, and hence future finances for the Mexican state, at the forefront of decision making. Having politicians with multiple constituencies (including the petroleum worker's union and companies that thrive off the oil supply chain) and short-term political considerations often make essential decisions is incompatible with the long-term planning needed in the oil sector. However, precisely because PEMEX can be a useful tool for political goals, achieving fundamental structural change is very difficult.

In sum, the authors agree that reform must happen to sustain and robustly grow Mexican oil production. The stakes of doing so are high for the Mexican Government. PEMEX directly provides 40% of government revenues, including significant resources transferred to the individual Mexican states. Decreased oil production has, thus far, been offset by higher than average global oil prices, but no government budget should rely so heavily on volatile commodity markets. While some commentators have argued that the budgetary pain of falling production would be useful to wean the budget from PEMEX, such a prospect could have wide repercussions on all programs funded in the Mexican budget, from poverty alleviation to the rule of law, let alone broader economic growth.

Natural Gas: An Emerging Priority

While oil provides vital government revenue, lack of natural gas development threatens to stunt Mexican industry. It is reported that parts of Mexico could face natural gas shortages in the coming year. Meanwhile, Mexico sits on a sea of unconventional natural gas reserves.

The current natural gas situation—which several interlocutors identified as a "crisis"—results from Mexican natural gas being priced artificially low because it is linked to the U.S. price, which has fallen with the rapid expansion of shale gas supplies. Yet the impact of U.S. supply on Mexican prices exists despite the limited physical integration of the two countries' physical gas markets. When combined with gas shortages in Mexico, this indicates the need both for more pipeline connections to the United States and for building out Mexico's domestic gas infrastructure. Doing so is made difficult, however, by confusion in the Mexican market where the downstream natural gas sector has been relatively liberalized while the upstream remains under the monopoly control of PEMEX. The lack of an appropriate price signal drives up demand while, reportedly, causing PEMEX to "shut-in" some conventional production due to lack of profitability.

Several interlocutors pointed specifically to the need for expedited pipeline construction to connect with Texas. Quick U.S. federal and state actions to permit pipelines could helpfully reduce short-term supply pressures in Mexico and help open new market opportunities for U.S. gas. Long-term economic growth in Mexico, however, is believed to be better served by development of its abundant domestic resources. As an analyst said, "You cannot build a future in Mexico based on cheap gas imports from the U.S."

The United States government estimates that Mexico has one of the largest shale gas reserves in the world at more than 680 trillion cubic feet (tcf) of technically recoverable reserves, although Mexico itself uses estimates as low as 140 tcf. Much of that shale gas is thought to be contained in an extension of the Eagle Ford formation that is already producing in Texas. PEMEX reportedly has drilled just a handful of exploratory wells, and with prices being held down by the United States gas boom, it has little economic incentive to invest heavily in shale in its own right, let alone the opportunity cost of that capital compared to much more lucrative oil. Absent natural gas pricing reform, it is unlikely that PEMEX will choose to invest heavily into shale gas.

Awareness of shale gas potential is growing in Mexico; at the time of the authors' visit, for example, the Mexican government was hosting a meeting of shale gas experts. Many interlocutors were carefully watching shale developments in the United States both in terms of direct job creation and in wider economic opportunities for power generation, chemicals, and manufacturing. Development of shale could be particularly helpful for economic growth in Mexico's northern border region.

The authors found that developing Mexico's shale gas reserves, as with technologically challenging new oil frontiers, will require energy reform to galvanize private investment, technology, and expertise. At the same time, an additional level of government capacity building will be useful to aid official understanding in the geology, economics, and environmental protections necessary for shale production. The U.S. State Department's Unconventional Gas Technical Engagement Program is well positioned to enable access to needed information, if the Mexican Government chooses to participate.

Most interlocutors were optimistic that gas reforms to allow private investment would come to fruition because natural gas is generally regarded to be less politically sensitive than oil. The most common fear of such a reform expressed by interlocutors was that if gas reform passed separately than oil reform, it could stunt momentum for the latter. Moreover, it is highly unlikely that a successful natural gas reform could be completely delinked from oil. Based on the U.S. experience, much of the profitability of shale gas comes from associated high-value liquids co-produced with the gas, so it seems unlikely that significant private capital will flow if liquids are not dealt with in reform.

Considerations in Oil Reform Policy and Politics[7]

There is no shortage of ideas for possible reforms both within PEMEX, the Mexican Government, and outside. As U.S. Senate staff who have themselves been part of an unpredictable legislative process, the authors will not speculate on the exact nature of reforms. Rather, U.S. interest lies primarily in assessing whether reforms will be meaningful and whether U.S. companies will continue to have access to provide goods, services, and investments to the Mexican sector regardless of the nature of reform.

The key marker for any reform capable of significantly improving Mexico's oil production horizon is whether that reform will produce IOC willingness to invest their capital and expertise. Interlocutors disagreed on the extent to which PEMEX acting alone or through service contracts can marginally increase production, but virtually none disagreed that multiple large-scale investments, particularly in deep water and Chicontopec onshore, will require external sources of capital and expertise.

PEMEX itself had recently embraced reform under the leadership of Juan Jose´ Suárez Coppel, PEMEX's former head. The stance of Emilio Lozoya Austin, Suárez Coppel's recently announced successor as sitting head of PEMEX, will be vital to understanding what kind of reform the Peña Nieto government is considering.

Under Suárez Coppel, PEMEX advocated a three step process by which PEMEX would gain financial autonomy, enable risk-sharing with IOCs and recapitalize PEMEX (which suffers under heavy debt burden, including large unfunded employee benefits), and, eventually, open the sector to concessions putting PEMEX in direct competition with IOCs. In other words, to undertake reforms that would move PEMEX to "run like a business" rather than an "economic development agency," as described by a senior official.

President Peña Nieto has several times echoed the call for internal PEMEX reform by indicating it might be more like Brazil's PETROBRAS. While no specifics have been offered, presumably that refers to the ability of PETROBRAS to directly raise capital and ceding a portion of government ownership. However, the PETROBRAS example is a tricky one. On the one hand, the company has global reach and laudable expertise. On the other hand, large discoveries of domestic oil in Brazil have precipitated increased political influence on the company's affairs.

Given the entrenched interests in keeping PEMEX itself viable, its key supply contracts in place, its union workers employed, and its funding for the government budget in place, it is unlikely that any reform option would significantly challenge PEMEX's dominance in its current areas of production onshore and shallow off- shore. However, PEMEX is not currently producing deep offshore and only marginally producing in Chicontepec. A frequently discussed legislative option would be to institute reforms for those two high growth potential areas, along with unconventional natural gas, so that PEMEX could concentrate in its zones of expertise.

Any number of management, regulatory, and financial reforms could be beneficial to Mexico's energy future, but putting oil production on a sustainable growth path will require IOC investment and expertise. Many interlocutors expressed that another incremental reform would not be worth the political effort; as one observer stated, "If there's anything we've learned on energy reforms in Mexico, it is that if reforms are incremental, they don't work." The 2008 reforms, for example, have received mixed reviews with some proponents pointing to subsequent deep offshore oil discoveries and opponents bemoaning politically-appointed but nominally independent board members lacking in accountability. Politically, however, most interlocutors credit the 2008 reform with helping to pave the path of public acceptance for bolder reforms now.

Large-scale IOC investment is likely to come to Mexico if those companies are able to "book" reserves with the U.S. Securities and Exchange Commission, a financial accounting that increases the value of the company, which does not exclude joint ventures with PEMEX. In some jurisdictions, that means taking ownership and marketing the physical barrels of oil, but other options may be viable, such as selling the IOC share of oil to PEMEX at the wellhead so that IOCs never physically take possession of the oil.

Mexico's need for oil and natural gas reform is widely acknowledged amongst leaders in Mexico. The primary question remains whether domestic political conditions will allow reform to advance. Oil has a privileged status in Mexican identity and politics akin to the third rail of Social Security in the United States: it basically works for now, is widely acknowledged to not work in the future, and any attempts to reform it may jeopardize a politician's future.

Newly sworn-in President Enrique Peña Nieto campaigned on reforming the Mexican energy sector and his new administration appears committed to follow-through on that promise. The political will to reform is evident; it is less clear whether President Peña Nieto will garner sufficient support within his Institutional Revolutionary Party (PRI), including overcoming possible union opposition, to pass meaningful reform.

Having achieved incremental energy reforms in 2008, the now opposition National Action Party (PAN) leadership appears poised to support broader oil and natural gas reform if offered by the PRI. Previously, some observers had raised concern that the PAN may hinder reform, as the PRI had done under the Calderón administration, to frustrate the new Presidential administration. In addition, some interlocutors indicated that the leftist Revolutionary Democratic Party (PRD) could attempt to undermine oil sector reform, including by staging public demonstrations against any initiative. While the general contours of political distinctions can be surmised even now, the exact lines of debate will be determined only when the government offers the actual scope of their proposed reform initiative.

It is evident that the current government budgetary reliance on PEMEX makes it extremely difficult to leave more capital within the company to make necessary investments. That will be all the more difficult since President Peña Nieto has made several campaign promises related to expansion of the social safety net in Mexico. Reportedly, for example, President Peña Nieto will reduce PEMEX's 2013 budget by over a billion dollars compared to expectation. If it is to come, financial autonomy for PEMEX will likely have to be tied with government fiscal reform measures.

It is extremely likely that President Peña Nieto will pursue oil sector reform. Enabling PEMEX to engage in joint, risking-sharing oil development operations is thought to be an essential goal of likely legislative proposals pursued by the Peña Nieto administration, and may be joined by liberalization in chemicals, refining, and related downstream activity. At the time of the authors' visit, opinion varied on whether the administration's reform goals could be accomplished legislatively or if constitutional amendment would be required, although the latter is conventional wisdom.[8] That choice may ultimately be resolved by vote counting. As a senior PRI leader said: "we have the will [for Constitutional amendment], but we are not sure if we have the votes."

TRANSBOUNDARY AGREEMENT

The Transboundary Agreement (TBA) provides a bilateral basis upon which both countries can develop the legal framework necessary for joint production of oil and natural gas reserves that extend across our national maritime borders in the Gulf of Mexico.

Secretary of State Hillary Clinton and Mexican Minister of Foreign Affairs Patricia Espinosa Cantellano signed the Transboundary Agreement (TBA), officially called the Agreement between the United States of America and the United Mexican States Concerning Transboundary Hydrocarbon Reservoirs in the Gulf of Mexico, on February 20, 2012, at Los Cabos, Mexico (see Appendix I for the text of the agreement). The Mexican Senate ratified the agreement on April 12, 2012, but the Obama administration has not formally submitted the agreement for passage in the U.S. Congress.

The TBA was negotiated pursuant to the 2000 Treaty on the Continental Shelf, which called for the U.S. and Mexico to establish a mechanism that transboundary oil and gas reserves would be shared equitably. At the time, concern that companies would drain Mexican reserves from the U.S. side of the border was, reportedly, a hot button political issue in Mexico. Upon conclusion of the 2000 Treaty, the U.S. put a moratorium on oil and gas exploration on the U.S. side of the maritime border.

It is widely acknowledged in both capitals that the TBA negotiations moved quickly in order to be completed in time for the ratification in Mexico prior to 2012 Congressional elections. Both PAN and PRI political leaders used their influence to gain support for the TBA, which the Mexican Senate ratified.

In the United States, the TBA stalled within the Obama administration despite support by key officials in the Departments of State and Interior. Prior to completing the agreement, the Departments of State and Interior participated in Senate Foreign Relations Committee briefings to discuss status of the negotiations; however, there was no consultation on specific text. The

SFRC Minority Staff appreciated candid assessments offered by lead U.S. negotiator Ambassador Richard Morningstar.

The Obama administration has not taken a position on the key question of whether the TBA is a treaty or an executive agreement, although the latter seems the administration's more likely preference. A treaty would be reviewed by the Senate Foreign Relations Committee and require the advice and consent of the Senate, demanding a two-thirds vote, for approval. As part of the treaty process, the resolution of ratification would be reviewed and amended in order to provide Congressional understandings on issues left unclear by the text of the TBA itself. Additional implementing legislation affecting the Department of Interior would also be required and need review by its committees of oversight.

An executive agreement would not require the two-thirds vote necessitated by a treaty, but instead it would be approved in the same form as a statute, requiring passage by majority in both the Senate and the House of Representatives. Legislation approving the agreement, necessary implementing authorities, and clarifications regarding certain provisions of the TBA could be subject to amendment, including by items unrelated to the TBA itself, thus possibly miring the TBA in other political fights.

Regardless of whether Congress considers the TBA as a treaty or executive agreement, Congressional hearings and thorough examination of the TBA and its implementing legislative proposals are needed. So far the Obama administration has declined to officially submit its proposed implementing legislation to the committees of jurisdiction for action through regular order.

Congress has a duty and interest in overseeing international agreements. That holds for the TBA since several provisions of the TBA invite scrutiny and clarification, even as the overall agreement is in the interests of the United States.[9] For example, TBA Article 16 establishes an "expert determination" that is binding whereas Article 17 establishes an arbitration mechanism without specifying whether the arbitration is binding. Both provisions could impact U.S. federal revenues, among other issues. In another example, the TBA is intended to improve environmental and safety protections, but the plain language makes no such guarantee.

Article 19, for example, instructs adoption of common standards, but that could mean effectively lowering U.S. standards in the border region if the Interior Secretary is given unrestricted authority to implement that section.

Why the TBA Matters

The centerpiece of the TBA is the mandate to establish so-called "unitization" agreements by which companies licensed by the United States and Mexico's state oil company PEMEX would jointly develop oil and gas reservoirs that have been discovered to extend across the maritime boundary. In effect, unitization agreements would work similarly to more well-known production sharing agreements (PSAs), whereby companies involved will jointly develop a project in order to spread risk given that deep water developments will cost billions of dollars each.

Given PEMEX's lack of experience in deep water, the most likely outcome is that IOCs licensed by the United States would operate the developments and utilize infrastructure based on the United States side of the border, which is more extensive than that of Mexico near to the area of operation. However, the United States does have an interest in PEMEX gaining expertise in operation in deep water in order to improve the integrity of potential PEMEX operated developments exclusively in Mexican territory.

A key difference between the unitization agreements envisioned under the TBA and traditional PSAs is that physical barrels produced will be allocated to the legal jurisdictions of the United States and Mexico, presumably in proportion to the amount of reserves found on their respective sides of the border. The Mexican barrels, presumably, will be property of PEMEX as a state entity and the U.S. barrels will be treated under standard terms of U.S. licensing in the Gulf of Mexico.

It is unlikely that, from the U.S. perspective, the TBA will meaningfully increase U.S. domestic oil production in the near term. The maritime border area is deep water and would require massive investments. Such investments are possible and should be encouraged by the U.S. government, however, it will take years to get through regulatory hurdles and normal project development needs. However, the TBA would unlock the maritime border region from moratoria, thereby offering long-term opportunities to increase U.S. domestic production. The TBA should be seen as a net positive to helping reduce U.S. dependence on imports from troublesome regions and boosting domestic economic activity, and therefore the TBA should be viewed as a benefit for U.S. energy security.

Benefits of physical barrels of oil produced are potentially much greater in relative importance on the Mexican side of the border, which is experiencing decline in key fields, and that would be substantially beneficial to U.S. interests in Mexican economic growth. As discussed above, Mexico needs new oil production. Developing deep offshore production would help diversify the Mexican oil portfolio, providing economic benefit to the Mexican state whether that oil is sold for export markets or used domestically. Moreover, having IOCs working with PEMEX to boost domestic Mexican production will provide useful commercial opportunities and, importantly, boost confidence that Mexico will have significant oil available to export to the United States. As a reliable, proximate, and friendly neighbor, Mexican oil imports support U.S. energy security.

The TBA contains numerous provisions in anticipation of disputes on allocation of resources under a unitization agreement and implementation of those agreements. Legal analysis of these provisions is beyond the scope of this report. However, it is apparent that lack of clarity on the legal status of the dispute resolution mechanisms should be of concern to the U.S. Congress. The Obama administration contends that the agreement's arbitration mechanism is not intended to produce binding decisions, however, that is not specifically provided for in the text of the agreement and would be different from arbitration mechanisms in many other international agreements.

The TBA further contains requirements of data sharing and notification of likely reserves between the United States and Mexico, opening the opportunity for increased government-to-government collaboration on strategic energy policy choices. Mexico and the United States are relatively less advanced in effective communication and linkages of our energy systems than we are in less politically-controversial economic areas. Improved ties can improve understanding and galvanize cooperation in often unexpected ways. In the immediate term, closer oil sector communication will be beneficial in case of accidents in the Gulf of Mexico or in case of significant disruptions to global oil supplies.

On issues of environmental protection and safety, the TBA envisions that the U.S. and Mexico in the geographic area under the agreement will have common standards and that regulators from both countries will have access to oil and gas development facilities with the ability to order shutdowns in both jurisdictions if necessary. The Obama administration contends that means that Mexican environmental and safety standards, and enforcement, will have to rise to U.S. levels. There is no guarantee that passage of the TBA will precipitate systemic improvement in Mexican environmental and safety enforcement, but any improvement is welcome by the Mexican safety regulator and should be welcomed in the United States given possible impacts of a spill on U.S. economic interests and quality of life.

Perhaps the most important U.S.-specific benefits of the TBA are three-fold.

First, the TBA will, for the first time, allow U.S.-listed IOCs to work in partnership with PEMEX, not including service contracts. Many observers are optimistic that the TBA is the metaphorical camel's nose under the tent, paving the way to broader reform in Mexico. There is no guarantee of such an outcome, however, failure for the U.S. to approve the TBA may put a drag on Mexican domestic energy reform momentum. The TBA helps demonstrate that Mexico's oil patrimony can be protected in a joint production regime with U.S. companies. It was suggested by some senior officials that passage of the TBA could help prompt broader domestic energy reform in Mexico.

Second, it is unlikely that the U.S. maritime border areas would be developed without the TBA, whereas a PEMEX official indicated desire to begin exploration on the Mexican side of the border. Potential U.S. opponents of the TBA may argue that given PEMEX's limited ability to explore in deep water, the real effect of the TBA will be to reduce IOCs' competitive advantages. In other words, the opposition argument could state, the U.S. should simply move forward with exploration since our companies have the capital and technology to move more quickly than PEMEX. That criticism neglects the reality that, over the long-term, the IOCs have a greater interest in investing throughout Mexican territory than they do in a sliver of U.S. area along the maritime border. Therefore, those IOCs would not risk enraging the Mexican government by, potentially, draining Mexican resources from U.S. territory. Thus, U.S. interests in increased safe and secure domestic oil production along the border will be best met with the TBA.

Finally, passage of the TBA would boost U.S.-Mexico relations on energy issues, which have traditionally lagged. Mexican officials roundly expressed support for the TBA and expectation for U.S. ratification in conversation with the authors. The political impact of not approving and implementing the TBA would set back U.S.- Mexican relations on energy specifically and more broadly. Each of our countries has hot button domestic political issues that take courage for political leaders to address. In Mexico, oil is one such issue, and members of both the PAN and PRI put their political weight behind ratification in Mexico. The U.S. not fulfilling its side of the agreement would, therefore, be seen as a violation of trust and could erode confidence. In the extreme, although unlikely, if Mexico proceeds with domestic energy reforms, U.S. companies could be shut out of certain opportunities until the TBA is ratified. However, bilateral benefits of approving the agreement do not require immediate passage; U.S. commitment can be demonstrated by the Obama administration formally submitting the TBA for Congressional approval and commencement of Congressional hearings.

There is reason to believe that the TBA can receive broad bipartisan backing in Congress. It would benefit bilateral relations, promote domestic oil production, and improve environmental protections in the Gulf of Mexico. Following normal Congressional procedure to ensure the agreement is vetted and implementing legislation is reasoned will benefit each of those goals. External proponents of the TBA will need to increase communication and advocacy to improve the likelihood of Congressional leaders acting on the agreement in the 113th U.S. Congress.

North American Energy Security

The United States and Canada are radically transforming global energy markets. Unconventional oil and natural gas has led to a renaissance in North American energy production. Alongside continued growth in renewable fuel and power sources and energy efficiency, the continent is poised to be functionally self-sufficient in energy. Mexico should be invited to join in the U.S.-Canada driven resurgence.

The impacts of the North American oil and gas powerhouse reach beyond energy markets. Low-priced American natural gas is encouraging job creation, industrial growth, and new trade opportunities. Increasing U.S. domestic oil production and trade with Canada will keep more American dollars at home. Regimes that use their oil and natural gas riches for intimidation and coercion, such as Venezuela and Russia, are seeing their petro-fueled power eroded.

Affordable and reliable energy supplies are critical to job creation and quality of life for citizens of the United States and for our allies Canada and Mexico. North America has long been a global leader in energy innovation, production, and market promotion. The geographical proximity of our industrial and population centers with our resource basins, integrated supply and transport chains across borders, and cultural closeness of our peoples has encouraged steadily increasing coordination and integration of North American energy, transport, and related infrastructure.

Maximizing the potential for oil and natural gas to promote economic growth and security across the continent will require continual improvement in policy communication, infrastructure rationalization, and regulatory harmonization between the U.S., Canada, and Mexico. Canada and the U.S. have largely integrated energy systems, but fissures over the Keystone XL pipeline approval process is an example of the need for even greater regulatory coordination. Comparatively, U.S.-Mexico energy coordination and integration is well behind.

Power sector reforms prompted by NAFTA demonstrate that a trilateral effort can have major results. Most importantly, key leaders from both the PRI and PAN in Mexico City are interested in making progress. Recently, President Peña Nieto wrote: "Together with the United States and Canada, [energy shifts] may well contribute to guaranteeing North American energy independence— something from which we would all greatly benefit."[10]

RECOMMENDATIONS FOR ENHANCING U.S.-MEXICO BILATERAL COOPERATION

U.S.-Mexico bilateral cooperation has improved dramatically in the last 5 years. Mexican sensitivities regarding their sovereignty are still present in government dealings. But today they don't prevent bilateral cooperation, as they did in the recent past. As evidence in this regard, we have seen a significant increase in Mexico's efforts to institutionalize and even expand cooperation among both civilian and military officials.

The willingness to improve Mexican cooperation with the United States is partly due to the trust developed through the successful partnership the U.S. and Mexican governments have built while working against drug trafficking organizations. The $1.9 billion Mérida Initiative through which the United States provides equipment, training, and technical assistance to support the Mexican government's battle against the narcotics trade and transnational crime has created a platform for greater bilateral cooperation.

Today, our two nations work closer than ever before. Yet, there are still new areas in which the bilateral relationship should improve. Interlocutors both from the then-existing Calderón administration and senior advisers to then-incoming Peña Nieto administration expressed a similar desire to expand cooperation in the bilateral relationship. One senior member of the then-incoming Peña Nieto administration expressed that it is time to move beyond tourism and drugs, issues which are so prominent in the bilateral agenda today.[11] Of course, the development of a contemporary, comprehensive immigration policy ranks high when broadening the agenda is discussed.

The U.S. is well positioned to increase dialogue and cooperation on energy security with Mexico (included in renewable power and efficiency, which were not part of this review, but which are areas where cooperation can move forward without significant political obstacles from the Mexican side). Key recommendations include:

1. *The U.S. should approve the Transboundary Agreement.* The Obama administration should formally submit to Congress proposed implementing legislation and/or resolution of ratification for the Transboundary Agreement and request Congressional review through regular order. Congress should then quickly establish a timetable for consideration of that proposal and approval of the TBA.

2. *The State Department should integrate oil and natural gas development into the bilateral agenda.* U.S. Embassy officials are well-versed in energy concerns. The commercial service is already active in promoting business relationships, and some agencies are building technical relationships. The newly established Energy and Natural Resources Bureau at the State Department is ably led by a former Ambassador to Mexico, Carlos Pascual, and the bureau is well-equipped to lead broad U.S.G. cooperation in areas such as shale gas, transparency, trade, supply emergency coordination, demand management, and infrastructure integration should the Government of Mexico wish to work with the United States.

3. *The State Department should encourage Mexico to partner in unconventional natural gas issues.* Mexico's tremendous shale gas potential offers it opportunity for local job creation, economic growth, and gains in its balance of trade. For the U.S., Mexican development of its shale could offer valuable commercial opportunities, produce additional valuable liquids, and strengthen North America's position in global markets. The State Department's Unconventional Gas Technical Engagement Program is a ready vehicle for improved cooperation.

4. *The administration should encourage Mexican adoption of international revenue transparency norms.* The Pëna Nieto administration has identified the need for increased government transparency and anti-corruption as a priority issue area across the government. The energy sector is not immune from public suspicion, but it is perhaps more complicated because any reform meant to bring international oil company investment must also overcome suspicion of the companies themselves, ingrained since nationalization of the industry decades ago.

An opportunity to directly build confidence in both the government and potential IOC investors would be for the Mexican Government to institute strong oil and natural gas revenue transparency measures. Public disclosure of revenues received by the government from IOCs and PEMEX allow citizens to better understand budgetary pressures on the government and demonstrate the value that Mexicans receive from IOC investment. Some countries have also found that revenue disclosure also presents useful checks and balances between ministries and can help improve tax collection.

Under the Cardin-Lugar Amendment, Section 1504 of the 2010 Dodd-Frank Act, IOCs would already have to disclose payments with the U.S. SEC if they invest in Mexico (PEMEX itself is not covered since it is 100% state-owned and operating only within Mexico). Internalizing that process domestically within Mexico would compound benefits with essentially no additional cost to IOCs. Additionally, Mexico could work with the voluntary Extractive Industries Transparency Initiative (of which PEMEX is a supporting company) to build capacity and confidence with civil society and industry.

5. *Further enhancing U.S.-Mexico offshore safety coordination should be a priority for the Obama administration.* An oil spill in the Gulf of Mexico is not contained by international boundaries, and the U.S. coast is particularly at risk given circulation patterns.

    Mexico is poorly prepared to enforce offshore safety, which would be of particular concern for U.S. coastal communities if large scale oil operations are developed in areas of Mexico close to the maritime border (as have been recent deep water discoveries). Comisión Nacional de Hidrocarburos (CNH), a Mexican safety regulator created in 2008, has only 60 employees and, at the time of authors' visit, had not received scheduled budget increases from the Finance Ministry. Most troublingly, CNH has not conducted a single offshore platform inspection. As a senior official stated, "We are running safety risks because of under investment in this agency [CNH]."

    Mexico's CNH and the U.S. Department of Interior's Bureau of Safety and Environmental Enforcement should enhance cooperation, including U.S. technical and logistical support for CNH-led inspections of Mexican offshore facilities, with reciprocal visits to U.S. facilities. Reciprocal visits will be particularly beneficial to build relationships between CNH and IOCs. The TBA offers one avenue to pursue such an arrangement, but this could directly be accomplished on an accelerated timeline given eagerness of CNH leadership.

6. *The State Department should offer technical assistance in pipeline security.* Theft of oil is a growing concern and can form a dangerous intersection with widespread security concerns related to criminal networks. In 2011, PEMEX detected 1,324 illegal taps. Approximately 3.35 million barrels were stolen that year, up a third from 2010, and costing PEMEX over a billion dollars.

7. *With Canada, invite Mexico to join a standing process for North American energy security planning.* Inevitable changes in Mexico's oil portfolio are significant for North American infrastructure planning. The most obvious change is in volume of oil. Yet, the type of oil is also likely to change. Large new deep offshore discoveries contain lighter oil than Mexico's conventional heavy Mayan product, whereas U.S. Gulf Coast refinery capacity is equipped with coking capacity for the heavier oil. If future Mexican exports are likely to be lighter than they have been previously, then investments in Gulf Coast refineries and infrastructure to connect U.S. and Canadian refineries will likely reflect that reality.

    Numerous trilateral initiatives have been focused on energy or included energy as a component part. With shifts already underway in U.S. and Canadian oil and natural gas production, and the high potential of Mexico, communication on energy security planning should be enhanced and formalized in frequent consultations. Consistent with each of their domestic planning, the U.S., Canada, and Mexico could jointly analyze resource availability, infrastructure needs, and regulatory needs to pursue mutually-beneficial strategic planning for North American energy.

To conclude, the potential benefits of the United States and Mexico working more closely on their respective national energy goals has never been higher. For the United States, thoroughly understanding Mexico's oil prospects is also vital for our energy security outlook. Mexico's energy future is in the hands of Mexicans. The United States can and should talk plainly, as a friend, and offer our robust partnership.

APPENDIX I.— TEXT OF THE AGREEMENT BETWEEN THE UNITED STATES OF AMERICA AND THE UNITED MEXICAN STATES CONCERNING TRANSBOUNDARY HYDROCARBON RESERVOIRS IN THE GULF OF MEXICO

The United States of America and the United Mexican States (hereinafter, "the Parties");

Considering that the maritime boundaries between the Parties were delimited by the Treaty to Resolve Pending Boundary Differences and Maintain the Rio Grande and Colorado River as the International Boundary signed on November 23rd, 1970 (hereinafter, "the 1970 Treaty") and the Treaty on Maritime Boundaries between the United Mexican States and the United States of America signed on May 4th, 1978 (hereinafter," the 1978 Treaty on Maritime Boundaries");

Recalling that the continental shelf in the Western Gulf of Mexico beyond 200 nautical miles was delimited by the Treaty between the Government of the United Mexican States and the Government of the United States of America signed on June 9th, 2000 (hereinafter, "the 2000 Treaty on the Continental Shelf");

Bearing In mind that the 2000 Treaty on the Continental Shelf recognizes the possible existence of hydrocarbon reservoirs that may extend across the continental shelf boundary established in that Treaty;

Recalling also that Article 5, paragraph 1, subparagraph (b) of the 2000 Treaty on the Continental Shelf provides that the Parties shall seek to reach agreement for the efficient and equitable exploitation of such transboundary reservoirs;

Desiring to establish a legal framework to achieve safe, efficient, equitable and environmentally responsible exploitation of transboundary hydrocarbon reservoirs that may exist along the maritime boundaries established between the United Mexican States and the United States of America in the Gulf of Mexico;

Recognizing principles that promote equitable and reasonable utilization of transboundary resources, and desiring to maximize the long term benefits from their exploitation, as well as to protect the resources of both Parties; and

Recognizing that this framework is intended to encourage the establishment of cooperative arrangements based primarily on principles of unitization, and further recognizing that additional cooperative arrangements may be developed outside of the framework of this Agreement and that such arrangements may also promote efficient, equitable, and environmentally responsible exploitation of transboundary reservoirs,

Have agreed as follows:

GENERAL PRINCIPLES

Article 1

Scope

This Agreement shall apply to cooperation between the Parties with regard to the joint Exploration and Exploitation of geological Hydrocarbon structures and Reservoirs that extend across the Delimitation Line, the entirety of which are located beyond 9 nautical miles from the coastline.

If any provision in this Agreement would require a Party to alter the terms of any License existing as of the date of the last notification provided under Article 22, such provision shall not apply in such case. Notwithstanding the foregoing, the Parties recognize that It Is in their interest that such Licenses be subject to all terms of this Agreement, and shall undertake good faith efforts to bring those Licenses under this Agreement.

Article 2

Definitions

For the purposes of this Agreement:

"Confidential Data" means any information or data, including Geological Information, of any type, kind or character, whether written or oral, disclosed by one Party to the other that Is not publicly available and which Information or data has been identified by the disclosing Party as confidentlaI;

"Construction and Operation" means the fabrication, Installation, laying, use, modification, maintenance, repair and decommissioning of Facilities and/or Pipelines;

"Delimitation Line" means the maritime boundaries In the Gulf of Mexico delimited in the 1970 Treaty, the 1978 Treaty on Maritime Boundaries and the 2000 Treaty on the Continental Shelf, and any future maritime boundary in the Gulf of Mexico delimited between the Parties, as agreed;

"Development" means those activities that take place following discovery and delineation of commercial quantities of Hydrocarbons, including, but not limited to, geophysical activities, drilling, platform design, fabrication and transportation, and installation of all Facilities, whether onshore or offshore, surface or subsea, and which are for the purpose of producing the discovered Hydrocarbons, whether on or off the Unit Area, excluding any activity related to Exploration or Production;

"Executive Agency" means the Agency of the Party designated to carry out the functions specified in this Agreement, as each Party may designate from time to time;

"Expert Determination" means the resolution of a dispute by an expert in accordance with Article 16 of this Agreement;

"Exploitation" means Development, Production, and all associated activities, including, but not limited to, workover, servicing, completion, maintenance, and decommissioning of wells in a Transboundary Unit, including treatment and processing of gas or liquids from and/or the injection, reinjection or storage of any substance used for or derived from the aforementioned processes;

"Exploration" means the search for Hydrocarbons Including, but not limited to, activities such as: (1) geological and geophysical marine and airborne surveys where magnetic, gravity, seismic reflection, seismic refraction, gas sniffers, coring, or other systems are used to detect or Imply the presence of Hydrocarbons; and (2) any drilling conducted for the purpose of searching for commercial quantities of Hydrocarbons or needed to delineate any Reservoir to decide whether to proceed with Development and Production;

"Facility" means any equipment, infrastructure or installation used for Exploration or Exploitation including, but not limited to, drilling vessels, fixed or floating platforms, platform installed drilling rigs, floating production systems, storage units, flotels, surface or seafloor well heads, Intra-field gathering Pipelines, Intra-field cables, and all the accessories necessary for well drilling, well logging, well intervention, well repair and well testing and includes any vessel used to transfer production from an offshore facility while it Is physically attached to the Facility;

"Facilities near the Delimitation Line" means any Facility under the jurisdiction of either Party within a distance of 15 statute miles from the Delimitation . Line or further for transboundary Pipelines, but excluding supply and support vessels;

"Geological Information" means geological, geophysical or geochemical Information and data resulting from Exploration or Exploitation, including, but not limited to, Information from drilled wells and interpretations derived from such data, and which, subject to its national law, may be disclosed by a Party.

"Hydrocarbon" means all oil and natural gas, regardless of form, including any mixture thereof, existing in or derived from natural strata;

"Hydrocarbon Occurrence near the Delimitation Line" means a detection of Hydrocarbons during drilling operations within 3 statute miles on either side of the Delimitation Line;

"Inspector" means any person authorized by the competent authority of either Party to carry out inspection activities relating to:

a) the Construction and Operation of Facilities related to a Transboundary Unit;
b) any metering system relating to production associated with a Transboundary Unit;
c) health and safety; or
d) protection of the environment.

"License" means the authorization issued by an Executive Agency to carry out Exploitation or Exploration In a given area, and for the Construction and Operation of a Facility. The term License Includes a "lease" issued by the U.S. Executive Agency;

"Licensee" means any person or entity holding a License;

"Permit" means any permit, authorization, consent or approval issued under the law of either Party, relating to the Exploration or Exploitation of Hydrocarbons and/or the Construction and Operation of Facilities and/or Pipelines;

"Pipeline" means a continuous conduit, complete with such equipment as valves for flow control, transmission platforms, compressor stations, and communications systems, for transporting Hydrocarbons, produced waters or other fluids and gases from one point to another, usually from a point in the producing field or processing plant to another Pipeline or to points of utilization or storage;

"Production" means those activities, excluding Exploration and Development activities, for the removal of Hydrocarbons from a Transboundary Reservoir, including, but not limited to, treatment and processing of Hydrocarbons or other substances, the injection, reinjection or storage of any substance used for or derived from such activities, enhanced Hydrocarbon recovery activities, transfer and export of Hydrocarbons to shore, and all operations associated with well intervention, repair, maintenance, servicing, re-completion, and workovers;

"Reservoir" means a single continuous deposit of Hydrocarbons in a porous and permeable medium, trapped by a structural or stratigraphic feature;

"Transboundary Reservoir" means any Reservoir which extends across the Delimitation Line and the entirety of which is located beyond 9 nautical miles from the coastline, exploitable in whole or in part from both sides of the Delimitation Line;

"Transboundary Unit" means a single geological Hydrocarbon structure or Reservoir which extends across the Delimitation Line the entirety of which is located beyond 9 nautical miles from the coastline, approved by the Executive Agencies for joint Exploration and/or Exploitation pursuant to the terms of a unitization agreement;

"Unit Area" means the geographical area described in a Transboundary Unit, as set out in the unitization agreement; and

"Unit Operating Agreement" means an agreement made between the Licensees and the unit operator that, among other things, establishes the rights and obligations of the Licensees and the unit operator including, but not limited to, the allocation of costs and liabilities incurred in and benefits derived from operations in the Unit Area.

Article 3

Jurisdiction

Nothing in this Agreement shall be interpreted as affecting the sovereign rights and the jurisdiction which each Party has under international law over the continental shelf which appertains to it.

Article 4

Activity Near the Delimitation Line

1) Within 90 days following the entry into force of this Agreement and annually thereafter, the Parties shall consult on Exploration and Exploitation activities carried out within 3 statute miles of the Delimitation Line. Such consultation shall include the exchange of all relevant and available Geological Information associated with and derived from such activities.

2) Notwithstanding the consultation set forth in paragraph 1 of this Article, and subject to its national law:

    a.   if either Party is aware of the likely existence of a Transboundary Reservoir, that Party shall provide written notice to the other Party within 60 days of the date on which such Party became aware of such likely existence;

    b.   if either Party has approved or its Licensee has submitted for approval a plan for the collection of seismic data in an area within 3 statute miles of the Delimitation Line, that Party shall provide written notice of such plan to the other Party within 30 days of the submission and, as applicable, approval of such plan;

    c.   if either Party has approved or its Licensee has submitted an exploration plan applicable to an area within 3 statute miles of the Delimitation Line, that Party shall provide written notice to the other Party within 60 days of the submission and, as applicable, approval of such plan;

    d.   if either Party is aware of a Hydrocarbon Occurrence near the Delimitation Line, that Party shall provide written notice to the other Party within 60 days of the date such Party becomes aware of such Hydrocarbon Occurrence;

    e.   if either' Party's Licensee has submitted a plan to drill a well, the wellhead or borehole any portion of which will be within 3 statute miles of the Delimitation Line, that Party shall provide written notice of such fact to the other Party within 30 days of the date such Party becomes aware of such plan; and

    f.   if any Licensee has submitted a plan for the Development or Production of an area within 3 statute miles of the Delimitation Line, the receiving Party shall provide such plan to the other Party within 30 days of the acceptance of the submission by the receiving Party of such plan.

Article 5

Determination of Transboundary Reservoirs

1) Within 30 days following receipt of a communication under paragraph 2 subparagraphs a or d of Article 4, the Parties, through their Executive Agencies, shall initiate consultations with a view to determine whether a Transboundary Reservoir exists. ThExecutive

Agencies shall request their Licensees to provide all Geological Information relevant to such determination and shall submit to each other all available Geological Information in their possession.

2) If the Parties have not reached a determination on the existence of a Transboundary Reservoir within 60 days of the deadline for initiating consultations in paragraph 1 of this Article, either Executive Agency may submit the issue to the Joint Commission.

3) During the consultations referred to in paragraph 1 of this Article and the pendency of further proceedings under Articles 14 through 17 of this Agreement, the relevant Executive Agency shall, subject to its national law, deliver quarterly reports to the other Executive Agency on Exploration and Exploitation activities or operations carried out by Licensees within its jurisdiction in relation to the potential Transboundary Reservoir.

EXPLORATION. AND EXPLOITATION OF A TRANSBOUNDARY RESERVOIR OR UNIT

Article 6

Unitization Agreement

1) Any joint Exploration and/or Exploitation of a Transboundary Reservoir or Unit Area pursuant to the terms of a unitization agreement must be approved by the Parties. Such joint Exploration and/or Exploitation shall be conducted pursuant to the terms of a unitization agreement negotiated and proposed by the Licensees and approved by the Executive Agencies. The Executive Agencies should develop one or more model unitization agreements for use under this Agreement.

2) The unitization agreement shall include, Inter alia:
   a) The identification of the limits of the Unit Area and that of any Transboundary Reservoir;
   b) The Identity of the Licensees and their respective participating interests;
   c) The methodology used to calculate the allocation of production;
   d) A development plan for the Exploration or Exploitation of the Unit Area, including the estimated number and timing of wells,

and a mechanism for delivery and approval of subsequent changes to such plan;

e) The effective date and term of the unitization agreement;

f) The Identity and appointment of the unit operator, the process for resignation and removal of the unit operator, and the process for appointment of a successor unit operator;

g) Provisions regarding the transfer of interests;

h) Provisions for an accurate measurement of production;

i) Procedures for ensuring accurate payments of royalties and other proceeds;

j) Safety and environmental measures to be taken under the national laws of each Party;

k) Provisions for appropriate information sharing between the unit operator and each Party;

l) Procedures for the redetermination of the allocation of production, including a. timetable or the events that trigger such redetermination.

3) Each Party shall require that, together with the submission of a proposed unitization agreement, its Licensee or the Licensees acting together through the unit operator, shall provide all available data required by a Party in order for it to review the proposed unitization agreement, and each Party shall ensure that such files and data are available to the other Party.

4) Each Executive Agency shall approve, approve with modifications or reject the proposed unitization agreement within 120 days of its receipt. Either Executive Agency may extend this period, provided that the total additional period for consideration shall not exceed 120 days. If after the end of the latest period applicable for consideration by an Executive Agency either Executive Agency has not approved, approved with modifications, or rejected the proposal, the unitization agreement shall be deemed to be rejected. At any point during the period contemplated under this paragraph either Executive Agency may refer the issue to the Joint Commission for its consideration within the remaining portion of the period.

5) Any amendment to an approved unitization agreement shall be subject to approval by the Executive Agencies. Each Executive Agency shall approve, approve with modifications or reject any proposed amendment within 30 days of its receipt. Either Executive Agency may extend this period provided that the total additional period for

consideration shall not exceed 30 days. If after the end of the latest period applicable for consideration by an Executive Agency either Executive Agency has not approved, approved with modifications, or rejected the proposal, the unitization agreement shall be deemed to be rejected. At any point during the period contemplated under this paragraph either Executive Agency may refer the issue to the Joint Commission for its consideration within the remaining portion of the period.

Article 7

Management of a Transboundary Reservoir Prior to the Formation of a Transboundary Unit

1) If it is determined as a result of consultations pursuant to paragraph 1 of Article 5 or following further proceedings under Articles 14 to 17 of this Agreement that a Transboundary Reservoir exists, and a unitization agreement has not been approved by the Parties, each Party shall take steps to facilitate Exploitation of the Transboundary Reservoir as a Transboundary Unit. Such facilitation shall include a prohibition by each Party on the commencement of production of such Transboundary Reservoir for a period from the date of determination of the Transboundary Reservoir to the end of the final period for consideration contemplated in paragraphs 2 through 5 of this Article, as applicable. If production of a Transboundary Reservoir has already commenced, the relevant Party shall take steps it deems appropriate under national law to provide that ongoing production does not unduly prejudice implementation of this Agreement.

2) If, six months following the date of determination of a Transboundary Reservoir or, alternatively, an earlier date on which the relevant Licensees have each notified the Executive Agencies that they have decided not to enter into a unitization agreement or a subsequent date agreed by the Executive Agencies in order to provide additional time for the Licensees to pursue a unitization agreement, a unitization agreement has not been approved:

    a. each Party shall require its Licensee, within 60 days, to submit a proposed unitization agreement and associated Unit Operating Agreement to each Executive Agency; and

b.   the Executive Agencies shall, within 30 days, jointly determine an estimate of the recoverable Hydrocarbons in the Transboundary Reservoir, under the original conditions of such Reservoir, on each side of the Delimitation Line, and jointly determine the associated allocation of production.

3)   If the Executive Agencies are unable to reach the determination set out in paragraph 2 subparagraph b of this Article, such determination shall be referred to Expert Determination.

4)   Following the receipt of both unitization agreements and associated Unit Operating Agreements under paragraph 2 subparagraph a of this Article, or the expiration of such period without the receipt by the Parties of both unitization agreements, and determination of the allocation of production under paragraph 2 subparagraph b or paragraph 3 of this Article, the Executive Agencies shall have 90 days to approve one of the submitted unitization agreements and associated Unit Operating Agreement, or an alternative unitization agreement and Unit Operating Agreement developed by the Parties. If no unitization agreement and associated Unit Operating Agreement has been approved at the end of this 90-day period, the Issue shall be referred to the Joint Commission for consideration. If no unitization agreement and associated Unit Operating Agreement has been approved within 90 days of submission of the issue to the Joint Commission, Exploitation of the Transboundary Reservoir may proceed pursuant to paragraph 5 of this Article.

5)   Should any Party or Licensee fail to sign a unitization agreement or Unit Operating Agreement, as applicable, approved by the Executive Agencies or the Joint Commission within 60 days of its approval, or should the Executive Agencies or the Joint Commission fail to approve a unitization agreement and an associated Unit Operating Agreement, each Party may authorize its Licensee to proceed with Exploitation of the relevant Transboundary Reservoir subject to the determination of the recoverable Hydrocarbons pursuant to paragraph 2 subparagraph b or paragraph 3 of this Article and any plan for joint management of the Transboundary Reservoir,Including any provisions agreed governing redetermination and metering, as may be agreed between the Parties. Such plan may contain provisions for the resolution of disputes pursuant to Article 16. In the event ofsuch Exploitation, Parties will exchange production data on a monthly basis.

6) The Joint Commission shall endeavor to resolve issues related to the allocation of production of a Transboundary Reservoir not otherwise addressed in this Article.

Article 8

Allocation of Production

1) The Executive Agencies shall require the unit operator, on behalf of the Licensees and 60 days prior to the commencement of production from a Transboundary Reservoir, to initiate consultations on the allocation of production to each side of the Delimitation Line by submitting a proposal for the allocation of production for approval by the Executive Agencies to be applied from first production. The Executive Agencies shall, prior to any decision not in agreement with the proposal, jointly consult with the unit operator.

2) Each Executive Agency shall ensure that all relevant and available information from the Unit Area related to the proposal Is made available in a timely manner to the other Executive Agency.

3) If the Executive Agencies are unable to reach agreement on this initial allocation of production within 30 days from the date of the initiation of consultations In accordance with paragraph 1 of this Article, the matter shall be addressed by the Joint Commission.

Article 9

Redetermination of the Allocation of Production

1) Any redetermination of the allocation of production of a Transboundary Reservoir shall be conducted pursuant to the unitization agreement or as agreed pursuant to Article 7 paragraph 5. The Parties shall endeavor to ensure that provisions for redetermination shall provide for fair and equitable allocation of production of each Transboundary Reservoir. Such terms shall be contained in the unitization agreement and shall be applicable over its full term.

2) Each Executive Agency shall ensure that, subject to national law, all relevant and available Information related to a redetermination of allocation of a Transboundary Reservoir is made available in a timely

manner to the other Executive Agency. The Executive Agencies shall, prior to any decision not in agreement with a redetermination proposal from a unit operator, jointly consult with the unit operator.

3) If the Executive Agencies are unable to reach agreement on any redetermination of the allocation of production within 60 days following the initiation of a process for redetermination as contemplated under paragraph 1 of this Article, the matter shall be addressed by the Joint Commission.

OPERATING AGREEMENT

Article 10

Unit Operator

1) The Executive Agencies shall ensure that a unit operator for a Transboundary Unit Is designated by agreement between the Licensees. The designation or change of the unit operator shall be subject to the approval of the Executive Agencies.

2) The unit operator will act on behalf of the Licensees.

Article 11

Unit Operating Agreement

1) Each Executive Agency shall require its Licensees to enter into a Unit Operating Agreement for the Exploration or Exploitation of a Transboundary Unit In accordance with this Agreement.

2) The Executive Agencies shall require that the Licensees submit an executed Unit Operating Agreement prior to the approval of the unitization agreement.

3) In case of a conflict between the Unit Operating Agreement and the unitization agreement, the unitization agreement shall prevail, or between the unitization agreement and this Agreement, the provisions of this Agreement shall prevail.

Article 12

Facilities Near the Delimitation Line
1) The Parties shall use their best efforts to facilitate cooperation between Licensees In activities related to the Exploration and Exploitation of a Transboundary Unit, including the facilitation of access to and use of Facilities near the Delimitation Line, and shall not prevent or impede such cooperation by unreasonably withholding necessary Permits.
2) The use of Facilities near the Delimitation Line may include, inter alia, access to and interconnection with a Pipeline and physical access to Pipeline capacity and, where appropriate, to Facilities supplying technical services incidental to such access.
3) The Parties shall facilitate, subject to their respective national law, access to Facilities for workers engaged in any activities related to a Transboundary Unit.

Article 13

Fiscal Terms
Income arising from the Exploitation of Transboundary Reservoirs shall be taxed in accordance with the legislation of the United Mexican States and the United States of America respectively, as well as the Convention between the Government of the United States of America and the Government of the United Mexican States for the Avoidance of Double Taxation and the Prevention of Fiscal Evasion with respect to Taxes on Income and Capital, signed on September 18th, 1992, as amended (and as may be amended in the future), or any Convention superseding that Convention as the Parties may enter into in the future.

INSTITUTIONAL ARRANGEMENTS

Article 14

Joint Commission
1) A Joint Commission shall be established no later than 90 days after entry into force of this Agreement to assist the Executive Agencies in administering this Agreement.

2) Each Party, through Its Executive Agency, shall appoint one representative and one alternate representative to the Joint Commission. Each Party may provide assistance,Including experts, to its representative as it deems necessary.

3) In exercising Its functions, the Joint Commission may establish working groups or expert groups, seek the advice of non-governmental groups or Individuals, and take such other actions as the Parties may agree.

4) The Joint Commission should endeavour to adopt its rules of procedure no later than 90 days after it Is established.

5) The Joint Commission shall be the competent body to examine any dispute or other matter referred to it by either Executive Agency relating to the interpretation and Implementation of this Agreement, or any unforeseen issues arising under this Agreement.

6) If the Joint Commission is unable within 60 days to resolve all differences concerning the allocation of production pursuant to Article 8, or the reallocation of production pursuant to Article 9,either Party may submit the dispute for Expert Determination. If the Joint Commission Is unable within 60 days to resolve all differences related to the determination of a Transboundary Reservoir pursuant to paragraph 2 of Article 5, and relevant data Is available from a well in the prospective Transboundary Reservoir on each side of the Delimitation Line, either Party may submit the dispute for Expert Determination.

7) If the Joint Commission Is unable within 60 days to resolve all differences concerning any dispute referred to It by the Executive Agencies relating to the interpretation and implementation of this Agreement that is not addressed in paragraph 6 of this Article or referred to It under paragraphs 4 or 5 of Article 6 or paragraph 4 of Article 7,either Party may resort to the dispute settlement provisions In Articles 15 or 17. The Joint Commission will have 30 days in which to consider the final recommendation in any arbitration Instituted pursuant to Article 17. If the Joint Commission is unable to resolve any remaining differences within that time, the dispute will be returned to the Parties.

8) The Parties will refrain from action with regard to any dispute referred to the Joint Commission or to Expert Determination or dispute resolution under this Agreement where it is reasonably foreseeable that such action would prejudice the Implementation of any decision

related to the dispute until the dispute resolution procedures are complete.

SETTLEMENT OF DISPUTES

Article 15

Consultations and Mediation

1) The Parties shall make every effort to resolve any disagreement relating to the Interpretation and Implementation of this Agreement through consultations as rapidly as possible. Either Party may initiate consultations through a written request to the other Party. Unless the Parties otherwise agree, the Parties shall consult within 20 days of delivery of the request.

2) If the Parties do not resolve a disagreement that is not subject to Expert Determination within 120 days of the delivery of the request for consultations, either Party may refer the disagreement to arbitration pursuant to Article 17 within 30 days.

3) The Parties may also agree to submit any disagreement relating to the Interpretation and Implementation of this Agreement to non-binding mediation by a neutral third party In addition to, or In lieu of, the procedures set out in this Article and In Article 17.

Article 16

Expert Determination

1) The Joint Commission shall, within 180 days of the adoption of its rules of procedure, establish arrangements for the appointment of the expert and terms of engagement, including, in particular, provisions governing compensation and the protection of confidentiality.

2) In the event a dispute is submitted to Expert Determination and the Joint Commission has not established the arrangements set out in paragraph 1 of this Article:

   a. each Party shall, within 30 days of the date of submission of the dispute and at Its own expense, choose an appointing expert.

    b.   the appointing experts shall, within 30 days, appoint the expert and determine the terms of engagement of the expert, including compensation, according to prevailing standards and strict protections of Confidential Data.

    c.   In such circumstances the costs of Expert Determination shall be shared equally by the Parties.

3)   Each Party shall promptly provide all information In its possession, or that it has the legal authority to obtain from Its Licensees, that exists and is required by the expert in order to reach a decision.

4)   The Parties shall ensure that the expert will maintain the strictest Impartiality and transparency. All communications between a Party and the expert, in any form, other than Confidential Data, shall be provided to the other Party.

5)   The Parties shall provide that, within 90 days of the expert's appointment, the expert will provide a preliminary decision to the Joint Commission together with a detailed explanation of how the decision was reached. Thereafter, there will be a period of 60 days, or such other period as the Joint Commission may agree, from the date that the preliminary decision is communicated to the Joint Commission during which either Party may seek clarification and/or make further submissions to the expert for his consideration. The final determination of the expert along with a detailed explanation shall be communicated in writing to the Joint Commission within 30 days of the end ofthis period.

6)   Notwithstanding paragraph 5 of this Article, the Parties shall provide that referrals to the expert under Article 7 paragraph 3 shall be resolved within 30 days of their receipt by the expert and that the expert's determination shall be provided directly to the Executive Agencies.

7)   Expert Determination proceedings will be confidential. Except as required by either Party's domestic law,the Parties shall treat, and shall ensure that the expert treats, any information provided for the determination, any written and oral communications related to the determination, and both the preliminary decision and final decision as confidential.

8)   Notwithstanding paragraphs 4 and 7 of this Article, upon any preliminary determination by the expert that a Transboundary Reservoir exists, all information used by the expert in reaching such determination and all information provided to the expert after such

date with respect to such Transboundary Reservoir shall be provided to both Parties. Such information shall be maintained as confidential by the Parties pursuant to the terms of this Agreement, subject to national law.

9) Determinations of the expert shall be final and binding on the Parties.

Article 17

Arbitration

If any dispute regarding the interpretation and Implementation of this Agreement that is not subject to Expert Determination cannot be resolved by the Joint Commission or through consultations, either Party may submit the dispute to arbitration. The Joint Commission shall, within 180 days of the adoption of its rules of procedure, establish an arbitration mechanism for the implementation of this Article.

INSPECTIONS, SAFETY, AND ENVIRONMENTAL PROTECTION

Article 18

Inspections

1) Subject to applicable national law, each Party shall, under procedures to be developed and agreed under this Agreement, have the right to inspect Facilities in a Unit Area approved pursuant to this Agreement.

2) To enable Inspectors of each Party to safeguard their respective interests with respect to safety, environmental and fiscal matters, the Executive Agencies shall develop specific procedures, subject to national law, for:

   a) consultation among Inspectors of each Party;

   b) timely access to Information relevant to Inspection activities; and

   c) physical access to Unit Areas for the purpose of inspecting activities therein under a joint inspection regime, including access to metering systems, wherever located.

3) The Inspectors of each Party shall act In cooperation and consult with Inspectors of the other Party to achieve compliance with applicable safety and environmental standards.

4) An Inspector of one Party may, with regard to Facilities located in the Unit Area, request an Inspector of the other Party to exercise his or her powers to ensure compliance with the applicable safety and environmental standards and requirements whenever It appears that circumstances so warrant. In the event of any disagreement between the Inspectors of the Parties, or the refusal of the Inspector of one Party to take action at the request of the Inspector of the other Party, the matter shall be referred to the Executive Agencies.

5) If it appears that it Is necessary for the purpose of averting risk to life or serious personal injury or significant damage to the environment, and that circumstances do not permit the Inspectors to consult with the Executive Agencies, the Inspector with jurisdiction over the activities giving rise to such risk shall, as authorized under national law, order the immediate cessation of any or all operations upon the request of the other Inspector. Immediately thereafter, but not more than 4 hours following the ordered cessation of activity, the Inspectors shall notify the Executive Agencies of such action and the reasons therefore, and the Executive Agencies shall Immediately consult regarding actions necessary to address the risk. Nothing in this paragraph shall prevent the right of each Party to authorize the resumption of operations of the relevant Facilities.

Article 19

Safety and Environmental Protection

1) The Parties shall adopt, where appropriate, common safety and environmental standards and requirements applicable to activity contemplated under this Agreement. In any event, the Parties shall strive to ensure that their respective standards and requirements are compatible where necessary for the safe, effective, and environmentally responsible Implementation of thisAgreement.

2) The Executive Agencies shall develop procedures for the implementation of this Article.

3) The Parties recognize the Importance of their existing international obligations with respect to oil pollution preparedness, response, and cooperation, and are to review their Implementation of such obligations in light of the activity contemplated under this Agreement In order to ensure an appropriate framework for ongoing cooperation.

FINAL CLAUSES

Article 20

Confidentiality
To the extent consistent with their national laws, the Parties shall maintain confidential, and obligate their Licensees to maintain confidential, all Confidential Data and other Information obtained from the other Party or its Licensees in accordance with this Agreement.

Article 21

Amendments
1) This Agreement may be amended at any time by mutual written agreement of the Parties.
2) Amendments shall enter into force in accordance with the procedure established under Article 22 of this Agreement.

Article 22

Entry into Force
The Parties shall so notify each other in writing when the necessary internal procedures have been completed to bring this Agreement into force. This Agreement shall enter into force 60 days after the date of the later notification.

Article 23

Termination
1) This Agreement may be terminated by mutual written agreement or by either Party at any time upon 180 days written notice to the other Party.
2) Notwithstanding termination of this Agreement, unless otherwise agreed by the Parties:
   a. the provisions of this Agreement shall continue to apply to any unitization agreement, Unit Operating Agreement, or other agreement entered into under this Agreement and in effect at the

time of termination, for the duration of such agreement, and to any such agreement submitted to or otherwise under review by the Parties pursuant to this Agreement at the time of termination, for the duration of such agreement;

b. the provisions of this Agreement shall continue to govern the relationship between the Parties with respect to any unitization agreement,Unit Operating Agreement, or other agreement entered into under this Agreement and in effect at the time of termination for the duration of suchagreements;

c. the provisions of this Agreement shall continue to apply to any License issued by a Party after entry into force and prior to termination of this Agreement;

d. the provisions of this Agreement shall continue to apply to the Exploitation of any Transboundary Reservoir undertaken pursuant to paragraph 5 of Article 7; and

e. the obligations of the Parties set forth in Article 20 concerning confidentiality shall continue to apply.

3) Upon any notice provided under paragraph 1 of this Article, the Parties shall initiate consultations for the development of a new agreement to address the joint exploration and exploitation of transboundary reservoirs.

Article 24

Termination of the Moratorium on Hydrocarbon Activity in the Boundary Area in the Western Gap of the Gulf of Mexico

Upon entry into force of this Agreement, the period of any moratorium on the authorization or permitting of petroleum or natural gas drilling or exploration of the continental shelf within the boundary "Area" as established by Article 4, paragraph 1, of the 2000 Treaty on the Continental Shelf and extended by any subsequent exchanges of notes shall be terminated.

Article 25

Relationship with Other Agreements

With the exception of Article 24, nothing in this Agreement shall affect the rights and obligations of the Parties with respect to other international agreements to which they are both party.

Done at Los Cabos on the twentieth day of February of two thousand and twelve, in the English and Spanish languages, both texts being equally authentic.

For the United States of America:
HILLARY RODHAM CLINTON
Secretary of State

For the United Mexican States:
PATRICIA ESPINOSA CANTELLANO
Minister of Foreign Affairs

End Notes

[1] The authors thank Clare Seelke, Curry Hagerty, Marc Humphries, and Angeles Villarreal of the Congressional Research Service for their background research. The authors also thank R. Chris Davy at the U.S. Embassy in Mexico City for his support of the staff delegation.

[2] Total U.S. imports have been trending downward since 2005, but imports from some countries are rising. In 2011, the U.S. consumed on average 18.8 million barrels of oil each day, down 2 million barrels from 2005. Despite that positive trend, the U.S. oil trade balance continues to worsen given increased global prices. U.S. Oil Imports and Exports, Neelesh Nerurkar, Congressional Research Service, April 2012.

[3] Mexico's oil and natural gas challenges are the subject of extensive commentary and scholarship. The authors recommend, for example, work by Lourdes Melgar of the EGADE Business School, Duncan Wood of ITAM, Miriam Grunstein of CIDE, and the Oil in Mexico series led by Amy Myers Jaffe of Rice University in partnership with the University of Oxford.

[4] Mexico Country Analysis Brief, United States Energy Information Administration, July 2011.

[5] Gasoline subsidies were reduced during the Calderón administration, but the overall cost of subsidy has risen given increased global oil prices.

[6] U.S. energy service contract companies are already active in Mexico.

[7] Given the political sensitivities of energy reform in Mexico, this SFRC report is only characterizing prospects for reform, not details. SFRC Members and staff wanting more detail should consult with Neil Brown or Carl Meacham.

[8] Article 27 of Mexico's constitution limits upstream ownership of hydrocarbons.

[9] The authors recommend that Committee Members and staff consult with SFRC Minority Staff Chief Counsel Michael Mattler.

[10] "U.S., Mexico should build on their economic ties," President Enrique Peña Nieto The Washington Post, November 23, 2012.

[11] Often underappreciated is that Mexico is the second largest trading partner of the United States with bilateral trade totaling $460 billion in 2011, up 16% over the previous year.

In: U.S.-Mexico Transboundary Hydrocarbons ...   ISBN: 978-1-63117-307-3
Editor: Hugh Bruner   © 2014 Nova Science Publishers, Inc.

Chapter 3

STATEMENT OF AMBASSADOR CARLOS PASCUAL, SPECIAL ENVOY AND COORDINATOR FOR INTERNATIONAL ENERGY AFFAIRS, U.S. DEPARTMENT OF STATE. HEARING ON "U.S.-MEXICO TRANSBOUNDARY HYDROCARBON AGREEMENT AND STEPS NEEDED FOR IMPLEMENTATION"[*]

Chairman Lamborn, Ranking Member Holt, and other Members of the Subcommittee on Energy and Mineral Resources. I appreciate the opportunity to appear before you today.

I know that each and every Member of this Committee is concerned about our nation's energy security, and I can assure you that Secretary Kerry and the Department of State share that concern. For that reason, I am happy to be here today to discuss the Transboundary Agreement between Mexico and the United States. The Administration supports the swift passage of legislation to allow for the implementation of the Transboundary Agreement signed by Mexico and the United States on February 20, 2012. We look forward to working with you on the legislation introduced last week to accelerate the safe

---

[*] This is an edited, reformatted and augmented version of a statement, Presented April 25, 2013 before the House Committee on Natural Resources, Subcommittee on Energy and Mineral Resources.

and effective development of hydrocarbon resources that cross the maritime border between Mexico and the United States.

Let me begin by stressing the importance that the State Department assigns to fostering a stable energy partnership with Mexico. Our energy trading relationship with Mexico is an important component of North American energy security as evidenced by the fact that Mexico is our third largest supplier of imported crude oil and the largest export market for U.S. refined petroleum products. It is also a growing market for U.S. natural gas exports. The Transboundary Agreement, by establishing greater legal clarity for the development of reserves that traverse the U.S.-Mexico border, would bring significant benefits to the United States and Mexico.

The United States and Canada have experienced an increase in energy production as a result of private investment, entrepreneurial ingenuity, technological innovation and strong commodity prices. U.S. oil production has increased by about 35% in the past five years. In contrast, Mexico has 10.2 billion barrels in proven reserves, but its production fell by 23 percent from 2004 to 2011, and projections forecast Mexican production will continue to decline in the short-term. This significant trend is often attributed to the maturation of major fields and the challenges for the national oil company, Petróleos Mexicanos (PEMEX), to maintain the necessary levels of investment in the sector. Mexican President Pena Nieto has made energy reform a priority, and if it is successful, Mexico could attract international investment and expertise to develop its hydrocarbon resources and reverse the decline in oil production. The Transboundary Agreement could be a down payment on the promise of more fundamental reform. Private investors would have a framework to develop cooperatively resources crossing the U.S. maritime border with Mexico. Such commercial engagement could capture resources that are currently not being developed because of legal uncertainty, and demonstrate that private investment produces resources and revenues that benefit the Mexican people and economy.

Despite the challenges facing Mexico in the near term, the exciting story here is that North American energy production as a whole could boost our respective national and global energy security. In North America, our energy resources give us the prospect to assure our energy supply. Just as important, North American resources will contribute to global market supplies, help balance global markets, and help promote the kind of stability in global energy markets that we need to support our domestic economic growth. Such opportunities, including the Transboundary Agreement between the United States and Mexico could support increased Mexican and North American production capacity and could be critical to world supplies and economic growth.

BACKGROUND

The Transboundary Agreement between the United States and Mexico addresses the development of oil and gas reservoirs that cross the international maritime boundary between our two countries in the Gulf of Mexico (excluding submerged lands under Texas jurisdiction).

The Mexican Senate overwhelmingly approved the Agreement in April 2012. The Administration has proposed legislative language that would provide the Secretary of the Interior the necessary authority to implement the Agreement, and this proposed language has been shared with the Subcommittee.

ROLE OF THE AGREEMENT

The Transboundary Agreement is an important step in our national efforts to better secure our energy future and at the same time promote a stronger and long-term cooperative relationship with Mexico in meeting each country's energy security goals. We believe the agreement would help facilitate the safe and responsible management of offshore petroleum reservoirs that straddle our maritime boundary and strengthen overall our bilateral relations.

The Agreement would enable meaningful energy sector collaboration between the U.S. and Mexico (and in particular between U.S. operators and PEMEX). We anticipate that this collaboration under the Agreement would provide U.S. operators with the ability to demonstrate the benefits of their participation in the Mexican energy market, potentially leading to deeper and more meaningful collaboration over time.

This Agreement will make nearly 1.5 million acres of the Outer Continental Shelf more attractive to U.S. operators by unlocking areas for exploration and development along our maritime boundary within U.S. jurisdiction. The Agreement would eliminate the moratorium on drilling along the boundary in the Western Gap, and provide legal certainty needed for investment in the boundary region outside of the Western Gap. It would allow American companies to enter into agreements – unitization agreements – with

PEMEX for the joint exploration and development of resources in specific areas. The development of a reservoir as a single deposit generally reduces the amount of drilling. Activities under unitization agreements would be required to comply with appropriate safety standards. As a package, these arrangements will potentially increase revenues and provide greater energy security, while mitigating safety and environmental risks that could result from unilateral development by each country along the boundary.

We are pleased that the Agreement would advance safety and environmental protection in the Gulf and provide significant safety and environmental benefits that would not occur without it. First, it provides for a system of joint inspections for all activity that takes place under the Agreement.

Though Mexican law would apply to operations under Mexican jurisdiction and U.S. law would apply to operations under U.S. jurisdiction, each side would have the ability to work with the other to ensure that all activity that takes place under the Agreement – wherever it occurs – meets all applicable laws and standards. In addition, under the Agreement our two countries would continue to work together to ensure that their respective standards and requirements are compatible where appropriate for the safe, effective, and environmentally responsible implementation of the Agreement.

In all aspects, the Transboundary Agreement offers the United States and Mexico significant benefits. It would, for the first time, establish a framework that would facilitate the development of hydrocarbon reservoirs that cross our maritime boundary with Mexico. This is a business friendly arrangement with strong safety and environmental payoffs.

H.R. 1613

We welcome H.R. 1613, The Outer Continental Shelf Transboundary Hydrocarbon Agreements Authorization Act that was introduced late last week. It is a promising step forward to implement the U.S. – Mexico Transboundary Agreement.

We support the goal of this legislation to grant the Secretary of the Interior general authority to implement the Agreement and to provide Congressional approval of the Agreement. We look forward to working with the Department of the Interior and the Committee on this important piece of legislation for expeditious approval.

CONCLUSION

In conclusion, we are encouraged by the accelerating pace of interest and movement on implementing this agreement. It is one that provides a much needed mechanism to facilitate the responsible and efficient exploration and development of hydrocarbon resources along the U.S.–Mexico maritime boundary. As many House Members have stated, it is a "win-win" for the United States and Mexico and also a winner for North American energy security because it fosters stronger relationships in the development of our shared energy resources.

I appreciate the time you and your staff are devoting to this issue and hope that we addressed to your satisfaction your requests for information on the many potential benefits for both the United States and Mexico, should the Agreement be brought into force.

Thank you again for this opportunity to testify before this Subcommittee and I would be pleased to answer any questions the subcommittee might have.

In: U.S.-Mexico Transboundary Hydrocarbons ...   ISBN: 978-1-63117-307-3
Editor: Hugh Bruner   © 2014 Nova Science Publishers, Inc.

Chapter 4

STATEMENT OF STEVEN GROVES, BERNARD AND BARBARA LOMAS SENIOR RESEARCH FELLOW, THE HERITAGE FOUNDATION. HEARING ON "U.S.-MEXICO TRANSBOUNDARY HYDROCARBON AGREEMENT AND STEPS NEEDED FOR IMPLEMENTATION"[*]

Mr. Chairman and members of the Committee,

Thank you for inviting me to testify before you today regarding the Agreement between the United States of America and the United Mexican States Concerning Transboundary Hydrocarbon Reservoirs in the Gulf of Mexico (the "Transboundary Agreement") and H.R. 1613, the legislation that has been introduced to implement the Agreement.

Developing hydrocarbon resources in the Gulf of Mexico along the international boundary with Mexico, including along the boundary within the "Western Gap" area on the extended continental shelf, is in the national interest of the United States. A successful implementation of the Transboundary Agreement advances that interest, and does so without entangling the United States in a deeply-flawed international convention

---

[*] This is an edited, reformatted and augmented version of a statement, presented April 25, 2013 before the House Committee on Natural Resources, Subcommittee on Energy and Mineral Resources

adopted more than 30 years ago—the United Nations Convention on the Law of the Sea (UNCLOS).

Proponents of U.S. ratification of UNCLOS claim that unless the United States joins the convention, it will be unable to develop the hydrocarbon resources in the Western Gap, including presumably any transboundary reservoirs. They claim that international recognition of the U.S. extended continental shelf (ECS), which is the continental shelf that extends beyond 200 nautical miles from the coast, is absolutely conditional upon U.S. accession.

However, that claim lacks basis in fact or law. The United States regularly demarcates the limits of its continental shelf and declares the extent of its maritime boundaries with presidential proclamations, acts of Congress, and bilateral treaties with neighboring countries. As a result of bilateral treaties between the United States and Mexico, the Department of the Interior's Bureau of Ocean Energy Management (BOEM) currently leases areas of the U.S. ECS in the Western Gap to American and foreign oil and gas companies for exploration and development. Indeed, BOEM has leased an area that sits directly on the international boundary within the Western Gap to Eni Petroleum, an Italian multinational oil and gas company.

The United States should take every action necessary—including the implementation of the Transboundary Agreement—to develop its hydrocarbon resources located on its ECS in the Gulf of Mexico. The United States can accomplish this end while acting as a sovereign nation rather than by joining UNCLOS and seeking the approval of the Commission on the Limits of the Continental Shelf (CLCS), an international committee of geologists and hydrographers located at U.N. headquarters in New York City.

The U.S. Extended Continental Shelf

Since 2003, in an effort to define the outer limit of the U.S. continental shelf, the United States has collected bathymetric and seismic mapping data on the outer margins of its continental shelf in the Arctic Ocean, Gulf of Alaska, Gulf of Mexico, and Bering Sea; along the Atlantic and Pacific Coasts; and off the Northern Mariana Islands, Kingman Reef, Palmyra Atoll, Guam, and Hawaii. The U.S. Extended Continental Shelf Task Force, an interagency project, is conducting this data collection.[1] To date, the ECS Task Force has identified six areas that "likely" contain submerged continental shelf and qualify as ECS and nine areas that "possibly" qualify. One area that likely contains ECS is the Western Gap, submerged continental shelf in the northern portion of the Western Gap. There is no evidence that any nation, any group of nations, or the international community as a whole does not or will not recognize the ECS in the northern portion of the Western Gap as subject to the jurisdiction and control of the United States.

Yet UNCLOS proponents commonly claim that U.S. companies will lack the "certainty" they require to develop the hydrocarbon resources located on the ECS unless the United States accedes to UNCLOS and receives the approval of the Commission on the Limits of the Continental Shelf (CLCS). For example, in 2007, former Deputy Secretary of State John Negroponte stated, "In the absence of such international recognition and legal certainty, U.S. companies are unlikely to secure the necessary financing and insurance to exploit energy resources on the extended shelf." Another prominent advocate of U.S. accession has argued that Proponents of UNCLOS offer no evidence that any foreign nation has not recognized or will not recognize the unilateral proclamations made by the United States. Yet the same proponents contend that the United States cannot hope to gain recognition of its ECS or assert jurisdiction and control over it unless and until it joins the convention. Law of the sea experts such as Ted McDorman at the University of Victoria disagree with that position:

> It can be asked whether a non-party to the LOS Convention can legally exercise jurisdiction over its adjacent continental margin beyond 200 nautical miles or whether this entitlement is only available to parties to the LOS Convention. The answer is that there appears to exist sufficient state practice...to support the view that, as a matter of customary international law, states can legally exercise jurisdiction over the continental margin beyond 200 nautical miles *irrespective of the State's status as a LOS Convention ratifier.*[3]

No evidence suggests that membership in UNCLOS is necessary, much less essential, either to gain international recognition of the U.S.'s ECS boundaries or to claim, legally and legitimately, jurisdiction and control over its ECS resources. It is telling that proponents of U.S. accession to UNCLOS do *not* claim that international recognition of the U.S. territorial sea, contiguous zone, or exclusive economic zone (EEZ) is contingent upon U.S. accession to the convention, yet they assert that accession is the *sine qua non* for international recognition of the U.S. ECS.[4]

There is no magic ritual for achieving international recognition of maritime and continental shelf boundaries. Foreign nations recognize and respect U.S. maritime claims and boundaries, and vice versa, as long as those claims and boundaries conform to widely accepted international law, including the various provisions of customary international law that are reflected in UNCLOS.

Like its other maritime claims, the United States will demarcate the limits of its ECS in a manner that conforms to international law. In November 1987, a U.S. government interagency group issued a policy statement declaring its intent to delimit the U.S. ECS in conformity with Article 76 of UNCLOS, which provides a formula for measuring the extent of a coastal state's ECS. The pertinent part of the policy statement reads:

> [T]he Interagency Group on Ocean Policy and Law of the Sea has determined that the proper definition and means of delimitation in international law are reflected in Article 76 of [UNCLOS]. The United States has exercised and shall continue to exercise jurisdiction over its continental shelf in accordance with and to the full extent permitted by international law as reflected in Article 76, paragraphs (1), (2) and (3). At such time in the future that it is determined desirable to delimit the outer limit of the continental shelf of the United States beyond two hundred nautical miles...such delimitation shall be carried out in accordance with paragraphs (4), (5), (6) and (7).5

Despite the claims of UNCLOS proponents, the United States can successfully pursue its national interests regarding its ECS—particularly hydrocarbon exploitation—without first gaining universal international recognition of its outer limits. While such recognition may be a worthy achievement, it is of no consequence to U.S. national interests whether the 195 nations of the world affirmatively recognize America's jurisdiction over its ECS in the Gulf of Mexico.

U.S. ECS IN THE GULF OF MEXICO

International cooperation on the delimitation of maritime boundaries is necessary in resource-rich areas such as the Gulf of Mexico. Since the 1970s, the United States and Mexico have negotiated a series of bilateral treaties to delimit their maritime and continental shelf boundaries, including areas of their abutting ECS in the Western Gap:

- In November 1970, the U.S. and Mexico signed a treaty to maintain the Rio Grande and Colorado River as the agreed international boundary between the two nations. As part of the treaty, the two nations demarcated their maritime boundaries in the Gulf of Mexico and the Pacific Ocean out to 12 nm.6 The treaty entered into force on April 18, 1972.

- In May 1978, building on the 1970 treaty, the two nations signed a treaty delimiting their maritime boundaries in the Gulf and in the Pacific out to 200 nm.7 The treaty demarcated boundary lines in the Gulf where their respective 200 nm EEZ abutted, leaving a "doughnut hole" of approximately 5,092 square nm (the Western Gap) where their 200 nm boundary lines did not meet. A second doughnut hole was created in the eastern Gulf where the EEZs of the U.S., Mexico, and Cuba fail to intersect (the "Eastern Gap"). The treaty entered into force on November 13, 1997.

- In June 2000, the U.S. and Mexico signed a treaty dividing the area of ECS within the Western Gap. Of the 5,092 square nm of ECS in the Western Gap, 1,913 (38 percent) went to the United States and 3,179 (62 percent) went to Mexico.8 The treaty established a drilling moratorium over a narrow strip along the international boundary within the Western Gap due to the possibility that transboundary hydrocarbon reservoirs are located along the boundary. The treaty entered into force on January 17, 2001.

Collectively, these treaties between the United States and Mexico, particularly the June 2000 ECS delimitation treaty, demarcated an area of U.S. ECS—the 1,913 square nm of submerged continental shelf in the northern portion of the Western Gap. There is no evidence that any nation, any group of nations, or the international community as a whole does not or will not recognize the ECS in the northern portion of the Western Gap as subject to the jurisdiction and control of the United States.

Yet UNCLOS proponents commonly claim that U.S. companies will lack the "certainty" they require to develop the hydrocarbon resources located on the ECS unless the United States accedes to UNCLOS and receives the approval of the Commission on the Limits of the Continental Shelf (CLCS). For example, in 2007, former Deputy Secretary of State John Negroponte stated, "In the absence of such international recognition and legal certainty, U.S. companies are unlikely to secure the necessary financing and insurance to exploit energy resources on the extended shelf." Another prominent advocate of U.S. accession has argued that U.S. failure to join the convention "could result in a loss of thousands of square kilometers of resource-rich...continental shelf."[9]

Reality tells a different story. The ECS area on the U.S. portion of the Western Gap has been available for development since August 2001. Specifically, BOEM offered the northern portion of the Western Gap for lease almost immediately after the 2000 U.S.–Mexico ECS delimitation treaty was ratified. That treaty entered into force on January 17, 2001. Seven months later, on August 22, BOEM offered the area of U.S. ECS in the Western Gap in Lease Sale 180. In that lease sale, three U.S. companies (Texaco, Hess, and Burlington Resources Offshore) and one foreign company (Brazil's Petrobras) submitted successful bids totaling more than $2 million for seven lease blocks in the Western Gap.[10]

U.S. Leasing Activity in the Western Gap

BOEM has offered the ECS blocks in the Western Gap in more than 20 lease sales between August 2001 (Lease Sale 180) and March 2013 (Lease Sale 227). In connection with those sales, seven U.S. companies (Burlington, Chevron, Devon Energy, Hess, Mariner Energy, NARCA Corporation, and Texaco) submitted bids to lease blocks in the Western Gap. Five foreign companies—BP, Eni Petroleum (Italy), Maersk Oil (Denmark), Petrobras, and Total (France)—also bid on Western Gap ECS blocks during those sales. BOEM collected more than $50 million in bonus bids in connection with lease sales on those blocks.

Of the approximate 320 blocks located in whole or in part on the Western Gap ECS, 67 (approximately 20 percent) are currently held under active leases by nine U.S. and foreign oil exploration companies.[11]

The successful delimitation and subsequent leasing of areas in the Western Gap demonstrate that the United States does not need to achieve universal international recognition of its ECS. The United States identified and demarcated areas of ECS in the Western Gap in cooperation with the only other relevant nation, Mexico, and that area was subsequently offered for development to U.S. and foreign oil and gas companies. All of this was achieved without U.S. accession to UNCLOS or CLCS approval.

Even though approximately 20 percent of the U.S. ECS that has been made available for lease by BOEM is currently under an active lease, the U.S. oil and gas industry has supported and will likely continue to support U.S. accession to UNCLOS in order to achieve even greater "certainty."[12] That is their prerogative, of course, and achieving a maximum amount of certainty is a legitimate and desirable goal for a capital-intensive commercial enterprise. However, the successful delimitation of the ECS in the Western Gap would appear to have provided the certainty necessary for several major U.S. and foreign oil companies to contemplate the development hydrocarbon resources on the Gulf ECS, including along the international boundary in the Western Gap.

The United States is unlikely to accede to UNCLOS in the near term, or perhaps ever. However, this does not mean that the United States should not take every action necessary— including implementation of the Transboundary Agreement—to secure oil and gas resources on its ECS in the Gulf of Mexico. The United States can accomplish this end while acting as a sovereign nation, continuing the tradition of American Presidents in proclaiming the nation's maritime and resource rights, and without acceding to a deeply flawed treaty or seeking the approval of an international commission of experts housed at the United Nations.

—Steven Groves is the Bernard and Barbara Lomas Senior Research Fellow in the Margaret Thatcher Center for Freedom, a division of the Kathryn and Shelby Cullom Davis Institute for International Studies, at The Heritage Foundation.

End Notes

[1] U.S. Department of Commerce, National Oceanic and Atmospheric Administration, National Ocean Service, "Extended Continental Shelf Project," revised August 25, 2011, http://continentalshelf.gov (accessed April 17, 2012).

[2] footnote text not available.

[3] Ted L. McDorman, "The Entry into Force of the 1982 LOS Convention and the Article 76 Outer Continental Shelf Regime," The International Journal of Marine and Coastal Law, Vol. 10, No. 2 (1995), p. 167 (emphasis added). McDorman cites evidence of actual state practice under the 1958 Convention on the Continental Shelf and UNCLOS Article 76 to support his conclusion.

[4] Besides the United States, other UNCLOS non-parties, including Cambodia, Colombia, El Salvador, Syria, Turkey, the United Arab Emirates, and Venezuela, delimit their maritime boundaries (e.g., 12 nm territorial sea, 24 nm contiguous zone, and/or 200 nm EEZ) in conformity with the convention without objection from other nations. See U.S. Department of Defense, Under Secretary of Defense for Policy, Maritime Claims Reference Manual, June 23, 2005, http://www.jag.navy.mil/organization/code_10_mcrm.htm (accessed April 17, 2012).

[5] "United States Policy Governing the Continental Shelf of the United States of America," November 17, 1987, reprinted in J. Ashley Roach and Robert W. Smith, U.S. Responses to Excessive Maritime Claims, 2nd ed. (The Hague: Martinus Nijhoff Publishers, 1996), pp. 201–202 (emphasis added).

[6] "Treaty to Resolve Pending Boundary Differences and Maintain the Rio Grande and Colorado River as the International Boundary," November 23, 1970, http://faolex.fao.org/docs/pdf/bi-51757.pdf (accessed April 17, 2012).

[7] "Treaty on Maritime Boundaries Between the United Mexican States and the United States of America," May 4, 1978, http://www.boem.gov/uploadedFiles/BOEM/Regulations/Treaties/1978_0504-TreatyMaritimeBoundariesMexicoandUS.pdf (accessed April 17, 2012).

[8] "Treaty Between the Government of the United States of America and the Government of the United Mexican States on the Delimitation of the Continental Shelf in the Western Gulf of Mexico Beyond 200 Nautical Miles," June 9, 2000, http://www.boem.gov/uploaded Files/BOEM/Regulations/Treaties/2000_0609-TreatyOCSinWGOMbeyond200nm.pdf (accessed April 17, 2012), and news release, "MMS Lauds U.S. and Mexico Continental Shelf Boundary Treaty Agreement," U.S. Department of the Interior, Minerals Management Service, June 13, 2000, http://www.gomr.boemre.gov/homepg/whatsnew/newsreal/2000/000713.html (accessed April 17, 2012).

[9] John Norton Moore, written testimony, in hearings, The U.N. Convention on the Law of the Sea (Treaty Doc. 103– 39), Committee on Foreign Relations, U.S. Senate, 108th Cong., 2nd Sess., October 14, 2003, p. 56, http://www.foreign.senate.gov/download/?id=564DC8D7-F536-4CCB-B0CE-3FD8A1C7CC6C (accessed April 17, 2012).

[10] U.S. Department of the Interior, Bureau of Ocean Energy Management, Regulation and Enforcement, "Western Gulf of Mexico Lease Sale 180 Information," updated August 30, 2010, http://www.gomr.boemre.gov/homepg/lsesale/180/wgom180.html (accessed April 17, 2012).

[11] U.S. Department of the Interior, Bureau of Ocean Energy Management, "Lease Sale Information," http://www.boem.gov/Oil-and-Gas-Energy-Program/Leasing/Regional-Lea sing/Gulf-of-Mexico-Region/GOMRHistorical-Lease-Sale-Information.aspx (accessed April 17, 2012).

[12] Paul Kelly, statement, in hearings, The U.N. Convention on the Law of the Sea (Treaty Doc. 103–39), pp. 113-116.

In: U.S.-Mexico Transboundary Hydrocarbons ...   ISBN: 978-1-63117-307-3
Editor: Hugh Bruner   © 2014 Nova Science Publishers, Inc.

Chapter 5

TESTIMONY OF ATHAN MANUEL, DIRECTOR, LANDS PROTECTION PROGRAM, SIERRA CLUB. HEARING ON "U.S.-MEXICO TRANSBOUNDARY HYDROCARBON AGREEMENT AND STEPS NEEDED FOR IMPLEMENTATION"[*]

Mr. Chairman and members of the Committee, good morning. My name is Athan Manuel, and I am the Director of Lands Protection for the Sierra Club. I am here representing more than 2.1 million Sierra Club members and supporters who belong to more than 65 chapters and 450 groups nationwide. We are the largest environmental grassroots organization in the country. I am very appreciative of the opportunity to testify this morning regarding H.R. 1613, the *"U.S.- Mexico Transboundary Hydrocarbon Agreement and Steps Needed for Implementation."*

The Sierra Club has always been a strong champion of protecting our special places and enjoying and exploring our planet, but we are equally concerned with issues of worker safety. We saw those two issues intersect 3 years ago last week when the explosion of the Deepwater Horizon off shore rig killed 11 workers and caused the largest oil spill in United States history.

---

[*] This is an edited, reformatted and augmented version of a testimony, Presented April 25, 2013 before the House Committee on Natural Resources, Subcommittee on Energy and Mineral Resources.

We see H.R. 1613 and the U.S. Mexico Transboundary Hyrdrocarbon agreement as a mixed bag. We support the idea of increased inspection of rigs operating in U.S. waters. However, we do not support the expansion of drilling into new areas.

We certainly agree with one of the goals of H.R. 1613, to promote domestic job creation, but think the best way to do that is by promoting domestic clean and renewable energy and energy efficiency.

I. INSPECTIONS

One goal of the Transboundary Hydrocarbon Agreement is to hold joint inspections of off shore drilling regulations The Sierra Club supports the reforms and regulations put in place by the Obama Administration, the Department of the Interior, the Bureau of Safety and Environmental Enforcement, and the Bureau of Ocean Energy Management in the wake of the BP Deepwater Horizon spill. Regulations that require operators to demonstrate that they are prepared to deal with the potential for a blowout and worst-case discharge, and mandating that permit applications for drilling projects must meet new standards for well-design, casing, and cementing, and be independently certified by a professional engineer per BOEM's Drilling Safety Rule.

We also support the guidance requiring a corporate compliance statement and review of subsea blowout containment resources for deep-water drilling. We hope all these standards will be applied to the nearly 1.5 million acres of the U.S. Outer Continental Shelf that could be leased as part of the Transboundary Agreement.

However, while these reforms have strengthened BSEE's inspection and oversight capabilities, funding levels remain far below what would be needed for frequent and thorough inspections. Low inspection rates not only undermine regulatory compliance by reducing the odds that violations will be observed, but also limit real-time monitoring of operations by inspectors. The explosion at the West, Texas fertilizer plant, which as last expected by OSHA in 1985, is one recent and vivid example. The best way to avoid another Deepwater Horizon spill is to increase monitoring and inspections, whether in areas currently open for drilling or the areas to be opened by the Transboundary Agreement.

Despite these tough new regulations, the U.S. lags behind the rest of the developed world when it comes to inspectors available and trained to inspect the oil and gas rigs off our coasts. The number of inspectors per offshore oil rig in other developed countries is as follows:

- In the U.K., the inspector to rig ratio is 1: 2.78
- In Norway, the inspector to rig ratio is 1:1.05
- In the U.S., the inspector to rig ratio is 1: 29[1]

We urge Congress to increase funding for BSEE's inspection program, and thus increase the inspection rate of our off shore rigs. Doing so would make these rigs safer and create jobs. The Sierra Club would support such an amendment to H.R. 1613.

II. CIVIL PENALTIES NEED TO BE INCREASED

The Sierra Club also feels that BSEE's civil penalties are too small to ensure compliance and deter risk taking by the oil and gas industry. The penalty for violating regulations is only $40,000 per day, per incident. Considering that the daily operating costs of a drilling rig can range up to $1 million, a $40,000 a day fine is not an adequate disincentive.

We feel that raising the maximum fine BSEE can assess for civil penalties to a level comparable with operational costs is warranted, and should be added to H.R. 1613 and applied to the area opened for drilling in the Transboundary Agreement.

III. APPLYING THE FINAL DRILLING SAFETY RULE

The regulations in the Final Drilling Safety represent positive reforms that are an improvement from the pre-Deepwater Horizon statutes. However, we feel that some improvement is needed, and that these improvements should be amended to H.R. 1613.

Improved maintenance and training are both positive reforms that can reduce chances of equipment failure and operator error and thus increase safety. Yet of all the provisions in the Final Drilling Safety Rule, training and maintenance regulations are the most dependent on the robustness of BSEE's oversight and inspection capabilities. Maintenance is an ongoing concern that necessitates being frequently checked and inspected and training is only valuable if it translates into appropriate actions, which also requires continuous oversight to ensure.

The Final Drilling Safety Rule requires drilling wells to be equipped with two independent barriers to flow. If correctly installed, these barriers could in fact protect against blowouts. However, the requirements for two barriers to flow can easily be undermined by operator error. This problem is illustrated by the Deepwater Horizon disaster, where a cement job, a common barrier to flow, was compromised by numerous operator errors. With limited funds for inspection and oversight, and perverse economics that incentivize project speed over safety, it is likely that not all barriers will be properly installed.

The Sierra Club hopes that the Fish and Wildlife Service and the National Marine Fisheries Service will be consulted before drilling activity begins in the areas opened by the Transboundary Agreement to review the potential impacts to endangered species.

IV. NO NEW DRILLING

The government's most recent Five-Year Plan allows access to more than seventy-five percent of the estimated undiscovered, technically recoverable oil and gas resources on the U.S. Outer Continental Shelf, including in fragile ecosystems like the Arctic.[2] That is clearly enough to keep the industry busy given that the oil and gas industry is sitting on a large number of inactive leases in federal waters, proving H.R.1613 to be unnecessary.

According to a March 2011, U.S. Department of the Interior report, oil and gas companies hold more than 4,000 leases for which exploration or development plans have not been submitted or approved.[3]

V. DOMESTIC ENERGY JOBS: CLEAN ENERGY VERSUS OIL AND GAS DRILLING

The Sierra Club strongly feels that the best place to create domestic energy jobs is by focusing on renewable energy and energy efficiency. The renewable energy industry is providing clean, affordable, and reliable electricity across the United States.

To support this industry, good green jobs are being created and they're overwhelmingly based here in the U.S. The sectors that heave demonstrated the most dramatic job growth are the wind, solar, and energy efficiency. In fact, every dollar invested in clean energy creates three times as many jobs as every dollar invested in oil and gas.[4]

Wind Industry

The security of federal tax incentives such as the Production Tax Credit (PTC) has brought wind manufacturing facilities to the United States, creating jobs and fostering economic development across the country. Today, the wind industry employs 80,700 Americans and there are over 400 facilities, in 43 states, which create parts for wind turbines.[5] These jobs are directly associated with wind energy project planning, siting, development, construction, manufacturing and supply chain, and operations.

Of the 80,700 jobs at the end of 2012, approximately 25,500 were in the manufacturing sector. Texas led the nation in wind jobs with over 10,000 employed in the wind industry followed by California, Iowa, Illinois, and Kansas.

The wind industry estimates that if the PTC remains in place, they will create 54,000 additional American jobs in the next four years, including 46,000 manufacturing jobs. This rate of growth would keep the industry on track to support 500,000 jobs by 2030.[6]

Solar Industry

For the third consecutive year, the U.S. solar industry continued its growth in 2012 and created jobs at a faster rate than the overall economy. As of September 2012, the solar industry employed 119,016 solar workers, a 13.2% growth in the solar workforce from revised figures for 2011. Of the nearly 14,000 jobs created in 2012, 86% of them are new jobs, rather than existing positions that have added solar responsibilities.[7]

The solar industry's growth is especially impressive given that the 12-month growth rate for the entire U.S. economy was only about 2.3%, which suggests that 1 out of every 230 new jobs in the U.S. economy was created in the solar industry this past year. During the same period, the fossil fuel electric generation industry shed 3,857 jobs, a decline of 3.77%.

Energy Efficiency

The effects of energy efficiency job growth are powerful and multi-faceted. Earlier this year, the Alliance Commission on National Energy Efficiency Policy (ACNEEP) unveiled its policy recommendations that were based on the bold yet achievable goal of doubling U.S. energy productivity.

An independent analysis of this proposal by the Rhodium Group found that doubling our nation's energy productivity by 2030 could[8]:

- Cut average household energy costs by more than $1,000 a year;
- Save American businesses $169 billion annually;
- Reduce government agency spending by $13 billion a year;
- Create 1.3 million jobs and increase GDP by up to 2%;
- Decrease energy imports by more than $100 billion annually; and,
- Reduce CO_2 emissions by 33 percent below 2005 levels.

Conversely, the Deepwater Horizon spill dramatically demonstrated how drilling can hurt coastal economies, cost rather than create jobs, AND reduce receipts to state and local governments and businesses. Pollution and spills from off shore drilling will damage booming and economically vital coastal tourism economies. According to the World Tourism & Travel Council, tourism in America employs over 14.7 million people, 10 percent of the American workforce, and accounts for 8.8 percent of the national GDP, bringing in $1.3 trillion. This makes America's coastal recreation and tourism industry the second largest employer in the nation. Our coast serves over 180 million Americans who make more than 2 billion trips to these areas every year. American tourism is a trillion dollar industry, and of that coastal communities alone contribute over $700 billion annually to our economy. Oil spills and pollution from rigs, whether they occur in the central and western Gulf, or in the areas opened by the Transboundary Hydrocarbon Agreement, are not compatible with our nation's tourism and recreation economies, our oceans and waters, or our coastlines.

End Notes

[1] "A review of the U.K. Safety Case Approach & Norway's Offshore Regulations" conducted by LCDR Marc Montemerlo, 2012.

[2] U.S. Department of the Interior. "Secretary Salazar announces 2012-2017 offshore oil and gas development program." 8 Nov. 2011. http://www.doi.gov/news/pressreleases/Secretary-Salazar-Announces-2012-2017- Offshore-Oil-and-Gas-Development-Program.cfm.

[3] U.S. Department of the Interior. "Oil and gas lease utilization – onshore and offshore." Mar. 2011.

[4] http://www.peri.umass.edu/fileadmin/pdf/other_publication_types/green_economics/ economic_benefits/economic_ benefits.PDF.

[5] http://www.awea.org/suite/upload/AWEA_USWindIndustryAnnualMarketReport2012_ ExecutiveSummary.pdf.

[6] http://www.awea.org/newsroom/pressreleases/Navigant_study.cfm.

[7] http://thesolarfoundation.org/sites/thesolarfoundation.org/files/NSJC%202012%20Factsheet% 20FINAL.pdf.

[8] http://www.ase.org/resources/energy-2030-impact-modeling.

INDEX